SUPERB CABINS

Edition 2007

Work conception: Carles Broto
Editorial coordinator: Jacobo Krauel
Graphic designer & production: Dimitri Kottas
Text: contributed by the architects, edited and translated by William George and Jay Noden

© Carles Broto i Comerma
Jonqueres, 10, 1-5, Barcelona 08003, Spain
Tel.: +34 93 301 21 99
Fax: +34-93-301 00 21
info@linksbooks.net
www. linksbooks.net

SUPERB CABINS:
"Small Houses in Nature"

LINKS

Index

Introduction

Architecture is the discipline that deals with space it works in space, from and with space. From an architectural point of view, this conditioning element is becoming increasingly scarce and paradoxically, the scarcer it is the more important its role in a project. The organization and optimization of space reveal an architect´s skill in response to the challenges of a limited space, a small site or a reduced budget. In this sense, architecture has been able to reinvent itself over and over, through the new construction and technological advances that appear on an almost daily basis. The idea of the primate "refuge", present at the gestation period of all small housing projects, leads into infinite dwelling possibilities that trancend the actual space and area available. Spatial optimization expands into the fields of versatility and the multifunctionality of constructive elements, including furnishing and instalations. This book provides a sampling of this ongoing architectural redefinition an overview of rural, traditional and experimental, weekend and permanent houses. In all their manifestations, they show that in architecture, reduced and compact doesn´t necessarily mean "limited". This extensively documented book presents complete detailed technical and graphic information for each project and its design process, from conception to completition. The internationally recognized architects contribute additional information and details of the solution adopted in each case. This combination provides a wide range of suggestions and useful examples that can help to define future projects. In short, an invaluable tool for all kinds of professionals and students of architecture and interior design.

Tom Kundig, Olson Sundberg Kundig Allen Architects

Delta Shelter

Mazama, Washington, USA

Photographs:
Benjamin Benschneider,
Tim Bies

Architects:
Olson Sundberg Kundig Allen
Architects

This steel box on stilts is a far cry from the log cabins of its owner's native Poland, but has all the benefits and more, being isolated on this 49 acre site in a dramatically beautiful landscape and yet eminently practical being both weather and vandal-proof. Situated in a 100-year-old flood-plain in the Methow Valley in the Cascade Mountains, Washington State this 1000 square foot weekend cabin rises on its sturdy steel stilts above the danger of the nearby river, and, despite its isolation, can be shuttered up like a safe when its owners return to the city.

Constructed in concrete and steel, the structure is held together by a welded and bolted frame of wide-flange sections. Many of the elements were made off site, then quickly assembled in the location. The materials make it virtually indestructible despite the harsh winters and threats of summer fires. The huge shoji-like shutters, measuring 10' x 18' are made out of 16 gauge hot-rolled steel sheets. They can be shut simultaneously thanks to a gear and cable apparatus operated with a hand crank, which in turn is a feature of the interior. The steel has been pre-rusted so, as architect Tom Kundig points out, it has a beauty of its own. Thus, despite its rugged, fabricated appearance, it blends surprisingly well into the environment (fitting in with the changing seasons, the autumnal hues and the bark of the trees).

On the ground level is a car port with an adjoining box that serves as a utility room and service area. Stairs lead up to the main entrance on the first floor which comprises a master bedroom with breath-taking views, a small guest room, a main bathroom and a smaller one. An internal wooden staircase leads to the main living area on the second floor, a sitting room and the kitchen which is enclosed in beech plywood. These two floors measure no more than 800 square feet in total, but the small interior is compensated by the immeasurable views. Designed to give maximum vision from within, half of each wall is glazed and the furniture and fittings are kept to a minimum. The plywood cladding on the walls, ceiling and stairs give warmth and lightness to the interior. The flat roof is slightly tipped, with windows running around it like a clerestory, allowing dramatic views of the mountain peaks.

For all its pragmatism this stunning weekend cabin set amidst the cottonwood trees is a wonderfully romantic 21st century tree house.

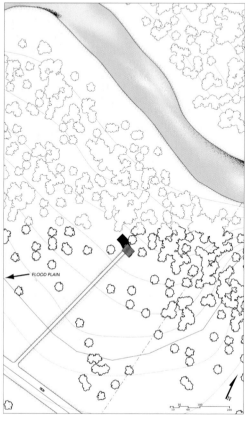

FLOOD PLAIN

▲ Tim Bies

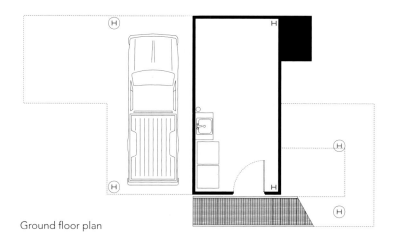

Ground floor plan

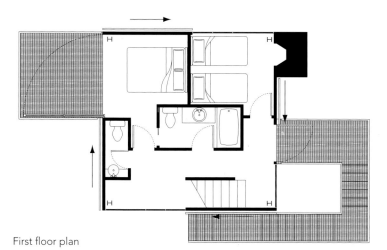

First floor plan

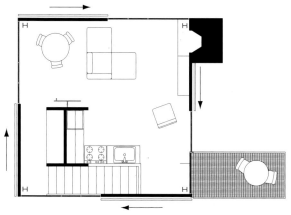

Second floor plan

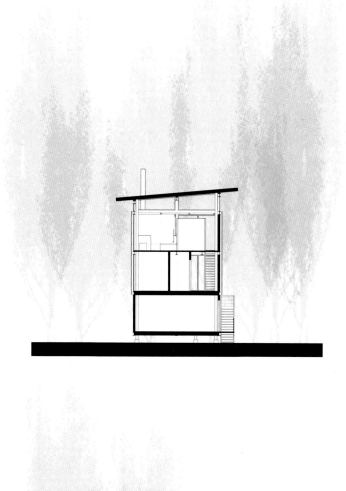

13

▲Tim Bies

The huge shoji-like shutters, measuring 10' x 18' are made out of 16 gauge hot-rolled steel sheets. They can be shut simultaneously thanks to a gear and cable apparatus operated with a hand crank, which in turn is a feature of the interior.

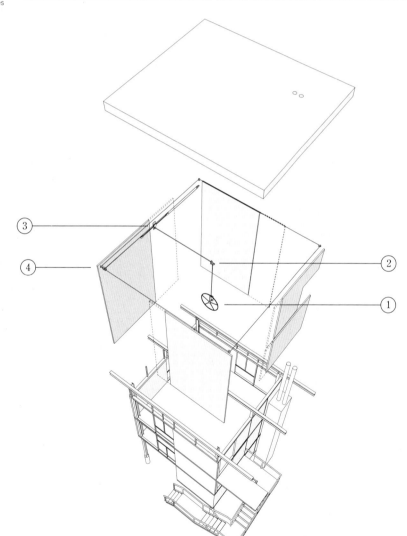

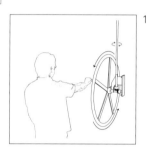

1

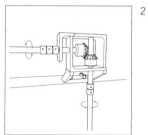

2

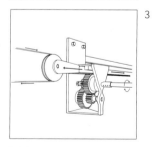

3

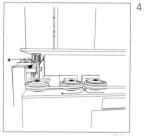

4

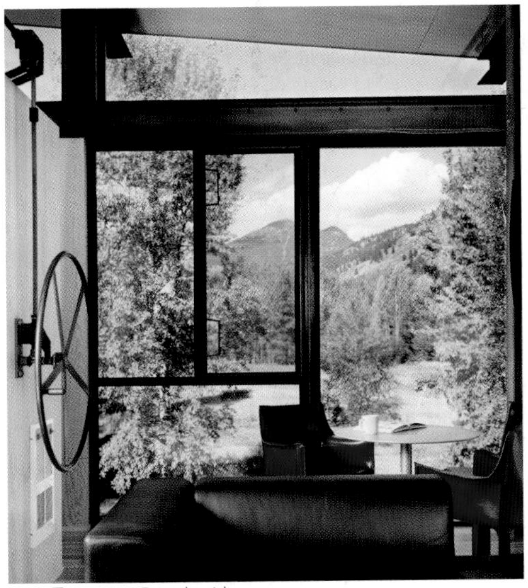

◀▲▶▼ Benjamin Benschneider

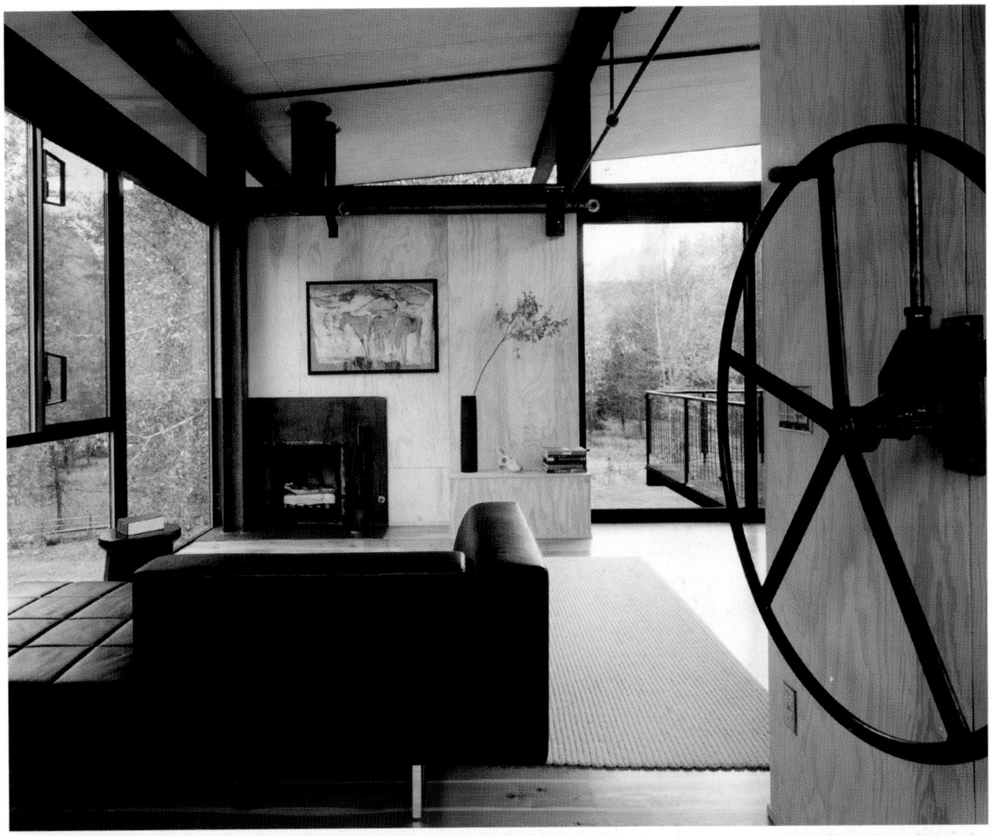

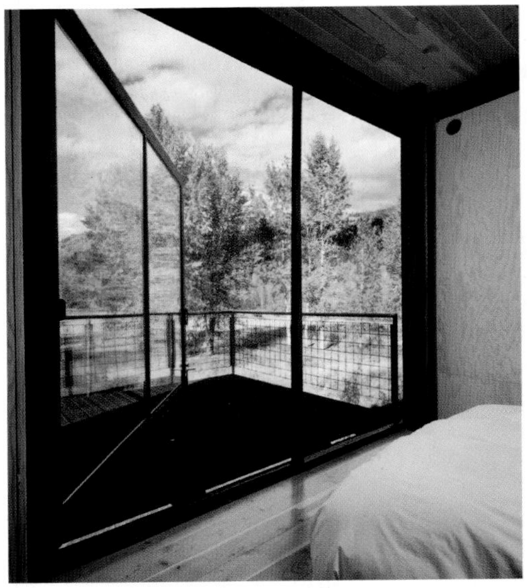

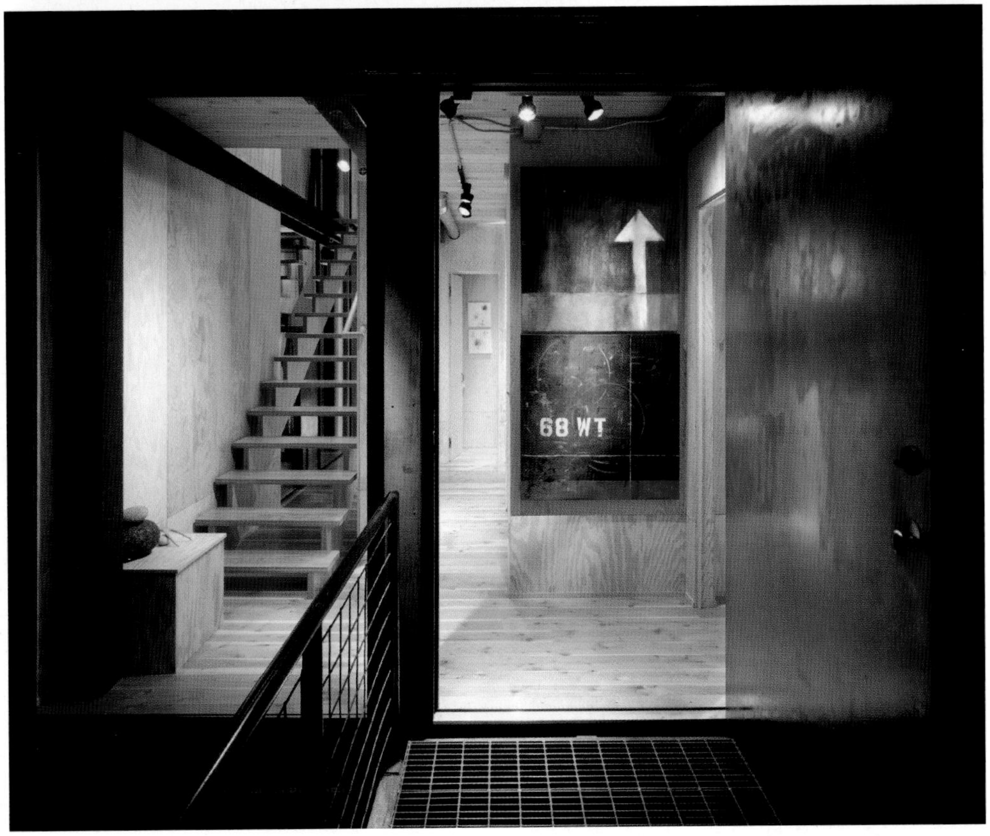

Nicholas Murcutt

Box House

Tanja, Australia

Photographs:
Brett Boardman

Architect:
Nicholas Murcutt

The Box House was designed by Nicholas Murcutt before the formation of Neeson Murcutt Architects, a small practice in Sydney, Australia, doing modest rural houses, bigger suburban houses and some urban infrastructures, occasionally collaborating with Neil Durbach, Camilla Block and Joseph Grech, on larger projects, while teaching and carrying out other professional tasks.

Environmental awareness and the peculiarities of each program drive the work. In the benign climate that characterizes the east coast of Australia, it is feasible to live partly outdoors for much of the year. As a holiday house, the Box House is free from the expectations associated with a primary residence, and offers the opportunity to question the notion of shelter, seeking to reconcile the spirit of camping with the comfort of modern living.

Set on an un-serviced rural site 500km south of Sydney, a single meeting between the architect and his artist clients established a mutual endeavor to re-interpret the 'shack' as a filter for the rural experience. As the distance of the site and a very modest budget precluded pre-construction site visits, the project was designed from photographs, the clients' notes and a basic site survey. The house was conceived as a prototype, a 6 × 6 × 6 m timber cube, a form chosen for its efficiency and its readability as an object.

Reminiscent of a rural barn, economy and clarity prevail over complexity, with a limited palette of locally sourced or recycled materials chosen for their associative qualities, physical durability and affordability. Entirely built of local Australian hardwood timbers and glass, the house combines one of the oldest building materials with a modern form, the cube. The solid timber doors and windows are integrated into the timber walls, to make the form, externally, as sheer as possible.

The clients set up an outdoor fireplace and bathtub that enabled them to camp on the site while their house was designed and built. These elements then remained in place and in use, so the house became an addition to the campsite, almost a 'hard tent.'

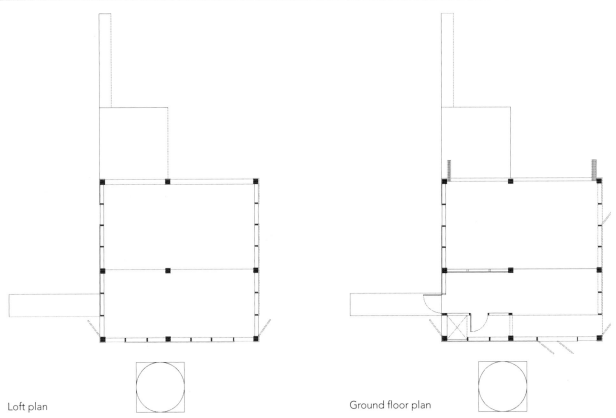

Loft plan

Ground floor plan

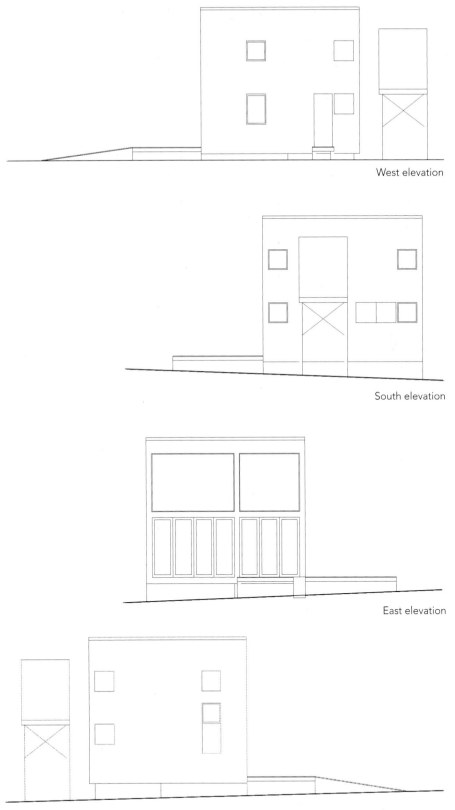

West elevation

South elevation

East elevation

North elevation

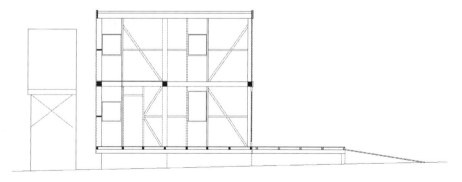

Entirely built of local Australian hardwood timbers and glass, the house combines one of the oldest building materials with a modern form, the cube. The solid timber doors and windows are integrated into the timber walls, to make the form, externally, as sheer as possible.

Schneider + Schumacher

Atelierhouse Nordeifel

Nordeifel, Germany

Photographs:
Jörg Hempel

The commission called for the creation of a small work cabin in the midst of the harsh climate of Nordeifel park. Set on a south-facing trapezoidal plot on the gentle slope of a hill on the outskirts of a small town characterized by heterogeneous constructions, the cabin enjoys uninterrupted views of fields and forests all the way to the other side of the valley.

The plot's trapezoid shape was adopted both in floor plan and in elevation, thus taking on a progressive widening at the same time as the height increases in alignment with its southward orientation.

The walls running parallel to the longitudinal limits of the site are completely enclosed. The entrance zone, partly painted black, has small north-facing windows, corresponding on the upper floor to the bedroom and, on the lower, to the bathroom and entryway. The south façade, on the other hand, is entirely glazed and links the main, double-height living room to the landscape.

The reduction to the minimum of surfaces and structures enhances the feeling of maximum space, which seems to project outward into the landscape.

In order to keep the impact on the surroundings to a bare minimum, a lightweight wooden construction that seems to hover over the muddy soil was chosen.

The surfaces of the three-layer prefab spruce panels for the floors, walls and ceiling were left untreated in the interior and only clad in bitumen sealing on the exterior. The limited budget and the future sporadic use of the house necessitated the use of simple, standard techniques, such as central wood-burning heating and exposed installations in the bathroom.

In spite of the considerable difficulties in getting the house approved by the City Council, since its construction it has been proved to be a choice spot for passersby and is appreciated by the townspeople and visitors alike.

Architects:
Schneider + Schumacher,
Frankfurt am Main
Project director:
Joachim Wendt
Collaborator:
Natascha Grap, Christina Flieger
Structural engineer:
Bollinger + Grohmann, Frankfurt,
Merz Kaufmann Partner für Kaufmann
Bausysteme GmbH, A-Reuthe
Mechanical engineer:
Raabe planen und beraten, Vallstedt
(EnEV-Nachweis)
Timber construction:
Barthel Korr GmbH, Aachen für
Kaufmann Bausysteme GmbH (GU)
Surface:
80.5 sqm
Building volume:
Height: 21,30 m
Length: 6,27 m
Width: 6,34 m
Cost:
130.000 €
Construction time:
July - October 2004

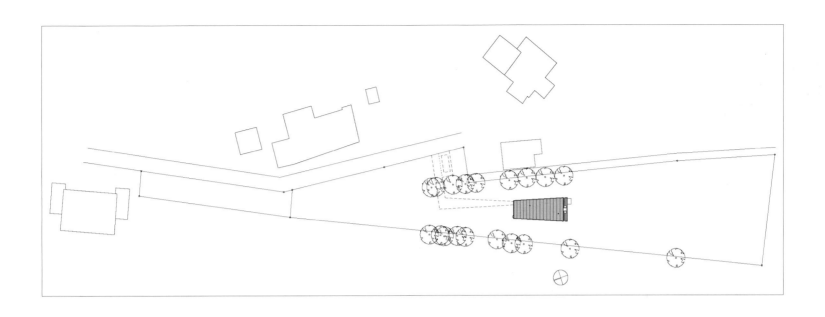

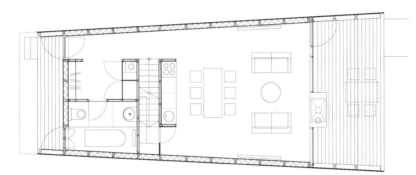

Ground floor

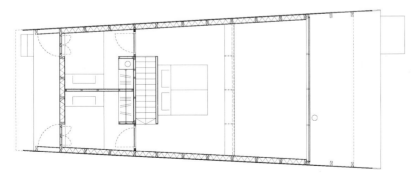

First floor

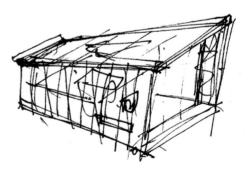

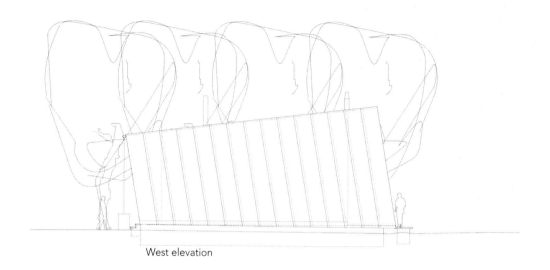

West elevation

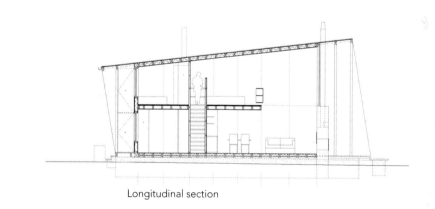

Longitudinal section

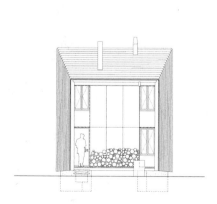

North elevation

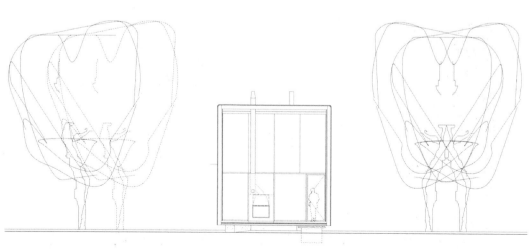

South elevation

In order to keep the impact on the surroundings to a bare minimum, a lightweight wooden construction that seems to hover over the muddy soil was chosen.

The south façade is entirely glazed and links the main, double-height living room to the landscape. The reduction to the minimum of surfaces and structures enhances the feeling of maximum space, which seems to project outward into the landscape.

Gwenael Nicolas , Curiosity

C-2 House

Yamanashi, Japan

Photographs:
Gwenael Nicolas

Architects:
Curiosity

The C-2 House stands in a thickly wooded area near Mount Fuji, a very special place for the Japanese. Located on a difficult, sharply sloping site, this retreat represents a dialogue with nature, framed by the environment's timeless performance. The temperatures range from 35 degrees centigrade in summer to minus 20 degrees in the winter, with 2 or 3 meters of snow. Such conditions determined the choice of a small but sturdy house.

Approaching the site through the forest was the seminal inspiration for the project. To enter the house one must first go through it, along a covered bridge to the opposite side where, still outdoors, it frames the striking view, perceived from the house as a chosen fragment of "borrowed nature".

The first impression, on arrival, is of a huge, abstract form, rising out of the ground and following the slope of the land downwards. It conveys a sense of tension, as if it were slipping. Is it moving? What stops it? In fact, the sharp angle of the building helps the load of winter snow to slide off the roof.

The covered bridge leads to the dining-room living-room kitchen, a 6m high space, like a mini-loft, that almost dispels the awareness of surrounding woodland. Light filters in from all around: long, invisible windows between the ceiling and the walls create an almost religious sense of peace and relaxation. As the outdoor conditions vary, the indoors atmosphere obeys a subtle choreography of light.

The interior lay-out enhances communication; people on the sofa remain in touch with people cooking: the kitchen floor is several steps down, so everybody shares the same eye-level. The kitchen counter conceals the stairs that lead down to the private areas in the basement, to where life in the house retreats at night; each room enjoys direct views of the forest. The seamless white bathroom seems to be a continuation of nature inside the house, especially when nature is covered by snow.

This sense of continuity guided the minimal palette of materials. The floors of the bridge and of the living room, as well as the aluminum roof, were stained the same dark color, so only the white walls are visible at night. Entirely built of wood, all the constructive details are concealed in the walls and the roof. Furniture is integrated in the design, and even the sofa is a continuation of the built-in shelving.

Entrance level plan

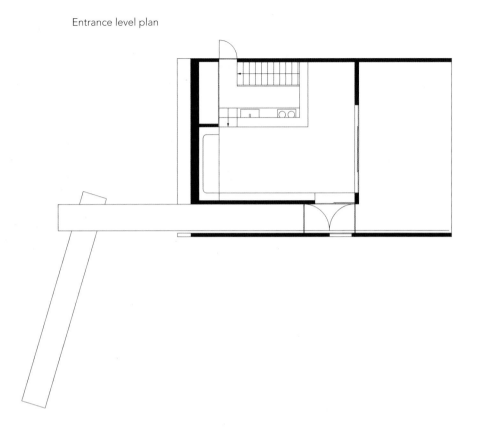

Lower level plan

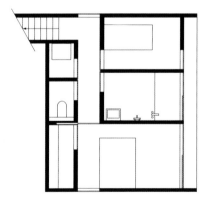

To enter the house one must first go through it, along a covered bridge to the opposite side where, still outdoors, it frames the striking view, perceived from the house as a chosen fragment of "borrowed nature."

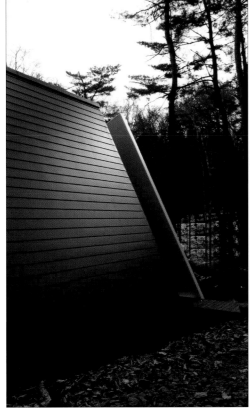

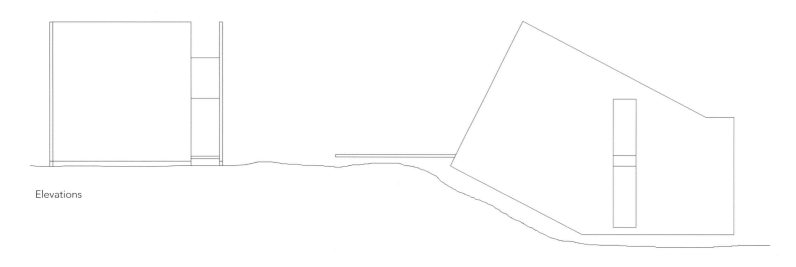

Elevations

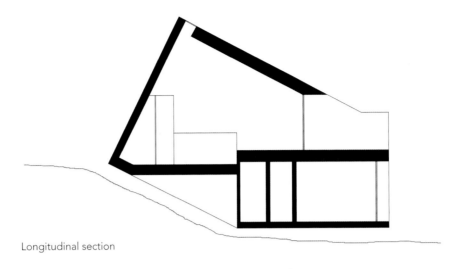

Longitudinal section

Light filters in from all around: long, invisible windows between the ceiling and the walls create an almost religious sense of peace and relaxation. As the outdoor conditions vary, the indoors atmosphere obeys a subtle choreography of light.

The seamless white bathroom seems to be a continuation of nature inside the house, especially when nature is covered by snow.

Drexler Guinand Jauslin

Weekend House

Pigniu/Panix, Switzerland

Photographs:
Ralph Feiner

Architects:
Drexler Guinand Jauslin AG

The village Pigniu/Panix is situated at 1300 meters above sea level, in the Surselva region of Graubünden, above Ilanz. The house is situated above the centre of the village. Although it is clearly a house of our time it is well integrated in the village's general appearance.

The building consists of two main floors, surmounted by a completely open third floor, merely enclosed by the two slopes of the gabled roof and by a sheer glass triangle at either end. A band surrounds the whole volume on its two main levels, concrete, for the plinth downstairs, wooden shingles for the upper living floor. The concrete band emerges from the landscape, to end at the street entrance to the house – from where the structure reads most clearly. A shift between the two levels articulates the volume's upper and lower halves, loosening the mass of the building and connecting it to the alpine environment. As fire regulations require a higher safety distance for wooden walls, the two upper floors stand partly shifted laterally off their concrete plinth.

The materials were chosen in accordance to the surrounding houses and barns. Its constructive language connects traditional and modern elements and techniques. The lower part is entirely of concrete with flat modular formwork – the upper part is of prefabricated wooden elements, clad with hand-cut larch shingles. The larch windows and shutters are the same for both parts – thereby accentuating the continuity of the band.

Despite its integrated exterior, the 150 sqm interior is distributed in a clearly contemporary manner, divided only by different levels and by sliding walls around the lower bedrooms. The continuity of the spiral is reflected in the spatial structure and determines the daily movement and flow of its inhabitants. The soapstone fireplace is the hinge of the movement, which continues throughout the three levels, from the stove to the "chaise très longue", to the kitchen.

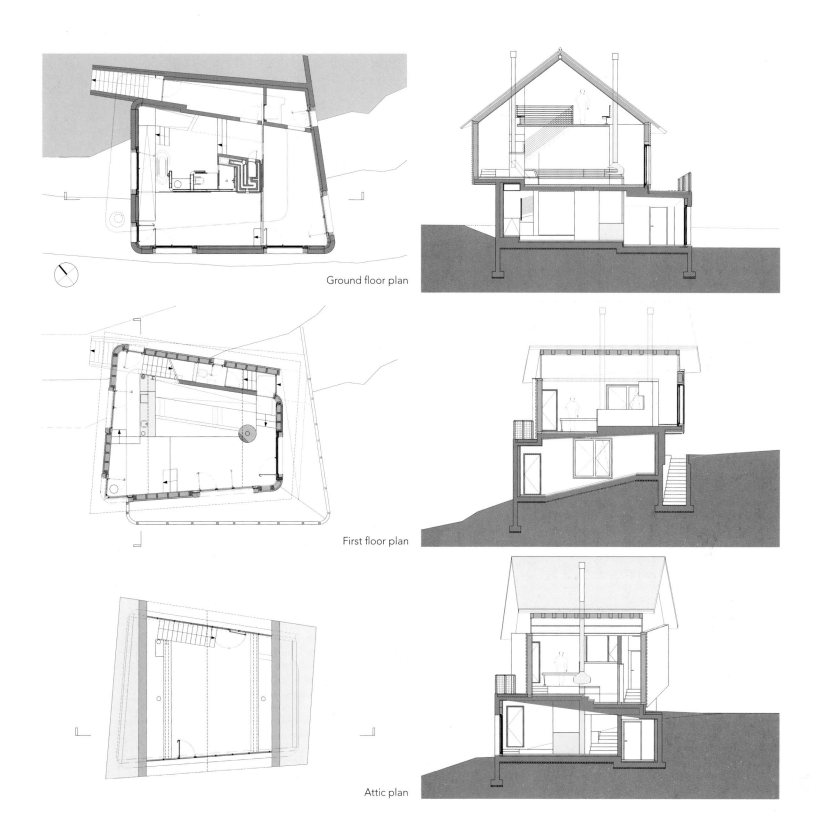

Ground floor plan

First floor plan

Attic plan

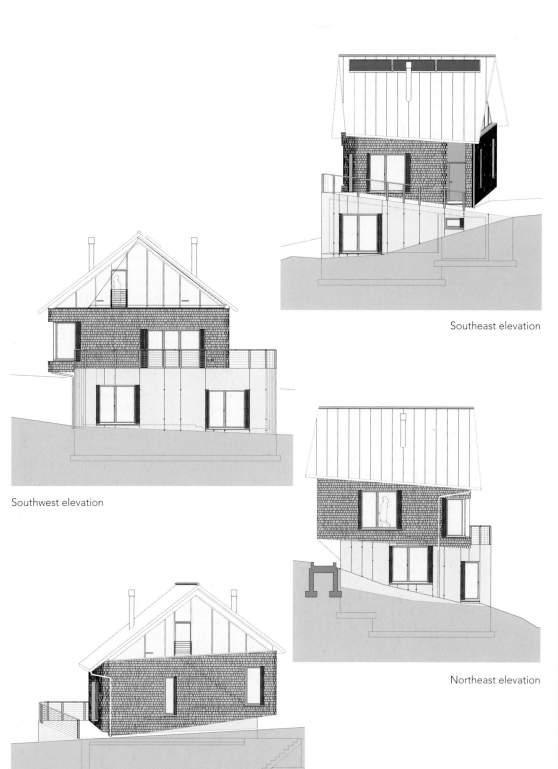

Southeast elevation

Southwest elevation

Northeast elevation

Northwest elevation

Lookout Cabin

Seeboden, Austria

Photographs:
Alastair Jardine

Architects:
Baumraum, Andreas Wenning
End of construction:
Summer 2004

A couple with children and eight grandchildren commissioned baumraum to construct a shelter for occasional use, respectful of the environment and affording its users the maximum enjoyment of the landscape. The result was the *Lookout Cabin*.

Situated in the Austrian region of Carinthia, the *Lookout Cabin* is a free-standing tower built on a steep hillside property, high above the town of Seeboden. Its supporting stilts, grounded in the hillside, rise through the surrounding trees to support two terraces, on different levels, and the "lookout cabin" itself, at the top. The *Lookout Cabin* is a dynamic-looking closed volume with a glass front aimed at the view of Millstäter Lake, the mountains in the distance and the rooftops of the village, shining through the trees by the shore. Wood is wonderfully responsive to light, and the building takes on different aspect as the weather and the seasons change, altering its visual relation to the location.

Completed in the summer of 2004, the *Lookout Cabin* serves as a play-area for the children, or a room for rest and relaxation for the adults, as well as a guestroom. The spacious terrace is large enough for a table and a few chairs.

Larch wood was used for the entire construction, including the board cladding. The weather resistant properties of this wood avoided the use of toxic wood preservers.

The side walls of the "Lookout cabin" consist of a structural timber framework, with an interior cladding of larch wood boards, over rockwool insulation and windfoil, and a ventilated exterior cladding of horizontal larch boards. The roof is kept watertight with asphalt sheeting.

From the lowest terrace to the top of the cabin's roof, the height varies from 3 to 8 meters.

To reach the *Lookout Cabin*, visitors must cross a ramp from the hillside to the lower terrace; from there, a solid stairway leads to the next level and then to the top. The interior design and space-saving yet comfortable furnishings resemble the interior of a small boat. There are drawers incorporated into the sofa-bed and a bench with enough space for blankets and anything else you might need. Simple interior lighting, some basic kitchen equipment and soft upholstery provide a cozy atmosphere with a touch of luxury.

Situated in the Austrian region of Carinthia, the *Lookout Cabin* is a free-standing tower built on a steep hillside property, high above the town of Seeboden. It is a dynamic-looking closed volume with a glass front aimed at the view of Millstäter Lake, the mountains in the distance and the rooftops of the village, shining through the trees by the shore.

Andreas Fuhrimann & Gabrielle Hächler

Holiday house on the Rigi

Rigi, Scheidegg, Switzerland

Photographs:
Contributed by
Andreas Fuhrimann &
Gabrielle Hächler
Architect:
Andreas Fuhrimann &
Gabrielle Hächler

The building has been situated in a peripheral position on the property, for the distance to the neighboring houses to be as large as possible and so that the option of constructing another building in the future would remain open.

The concrete cellar anchors the building into the sloping terrain and houses the entrance area and the technical and service rooms. Resting upon the stability of this plinth is the upper volume of the building, the footprint of which has a somewhat ship-like outline. This floor (ground floor on the side facing the slope) juts out eastward to a sufficient degree for a sheltered, protected, access area to be available, underneath the eaves.

The concrete chimney of the open fireplace rises like a mast out of the cellar and, together with a concrete wall, forms the bracing backbone behind which the two single-flight staircases connect the three floors. On the ground floor is a large living room spread over two different levels and with different ceiling heights. The deliberately low area in which the kitchen is contained creates a spatial feeling reminiscent of the sensation generated in the low parlors of the mountain cabins typical of local vernacular architecture. The 5-meter long fixed panorama window that frames the breathtaking view, perhaps the location's main asset, introduces a contemporary feeling of modernity.

The polygonal floorplan allows the space to be divided into areas of subtly unusual proportions, which enhance the characteristics of the building and contribute to a refreshing perception of novelty within the timeless and spectacular scenery of the Alps. Moreover, the open fireplace is granted a suitably predominant position, at the widest spot in the room.

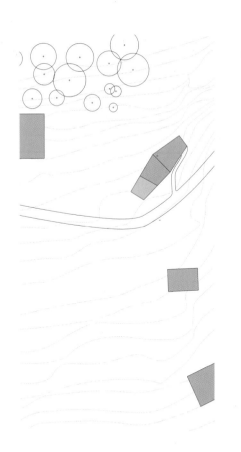

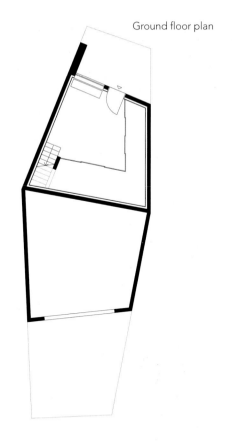

Ground floor plan

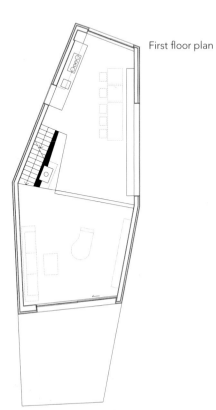

First floor plan

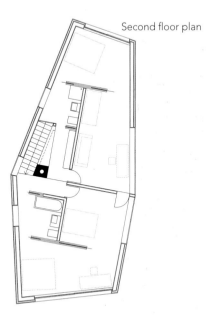

Second floor plan

65

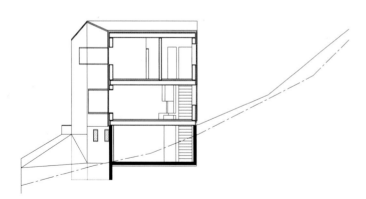

Cross section

Longitudinal section

North East elevation

North West elevation

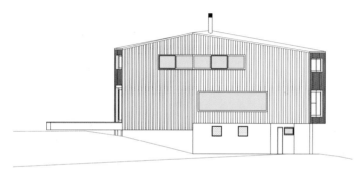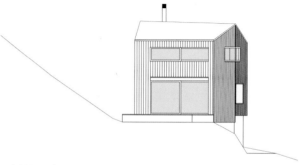

South East elevation

South West elevation

Helin & Co Architects

Villa Tuulentupa

Litti, Finland

Photographs:
Voitto Niemelä & Pekka Helin

Architects:
Helin & Co Architects
Construction end:
2003

A summer cottage, built in the 1960s on a rocky promontory in the vicinity of the village of Litti, had become a dearly beloved holiday home for three generations of the family that built it, but was required a profound renovation.

This long-term relationship created a clear basis for a harmonious solution. The family's own business activities have made them world citizens, and the aim was to create a home base in the midst of the best of the Finnish countryside – a place of rest but also one which functions as a generator of renewal and a meeting place for friends and relatives. Family friends include well-known foreign artists who can thus be offered a unique experience surrounded by nature.

The main view from the house opens on to the lake. Carved by the glaciers, the promontory's unusually beautiful rocks descend towards the water. On them grows an exceptionally diverse range of lichens, which cover the stone with a bewitching coloration. The sun encircles the promontory, from sunrise to sunset. Stunted spruces grow in the sparse earth, surrounded by great erratic boulders. The landscape enthralls the viewer with an unrelenting fascination.

The formation of the haphazard rocky environment is so strong that an orthogonal spatial distribution was not viable; instead, the free-form floor plan of the house arose from the morphology of the terrain itself.

The solution is a flowing space which moves from the main room to the bedrooms and out to the free form of the terraces, which open out in three directions. Smaller windows face the direction of approach, to which the house turns its back, as it does towards the neighboring plots. Instead, the house takes the lakeside terrace in its embrace. For people sitting on the terrace, the view of the lake is reflected in the great glazed openings, creating a 360-degree panorama of nature.

The house has been fitted into the natural scenery so as to disturb nature as little as possible, and the building lies in the land as though it had always been there; although the building's formal vocabulary has few overtly organic references about it, the result seems perfectly appropriate without making a self conscious effort.

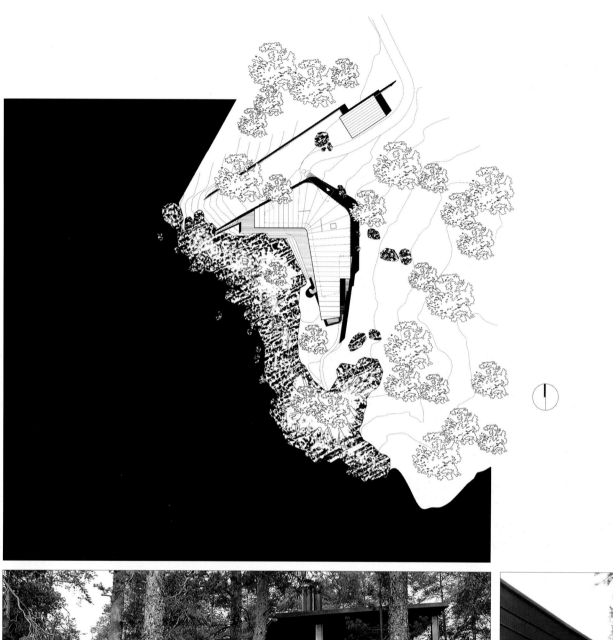

The predominant materials are wood and copper. The dark color of the copper merges naturally with the bark of the old spruces and the silver-grey planks blend with the ice-carved rock.

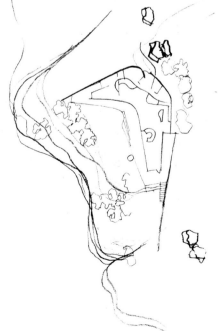

North elevation

West elevation

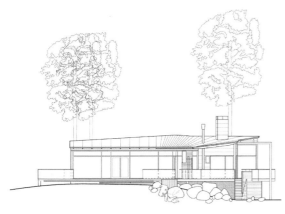

South elevation

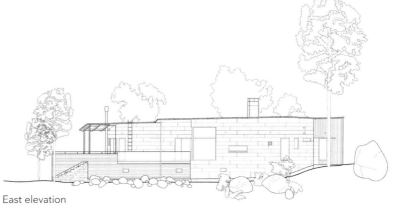

East elevation

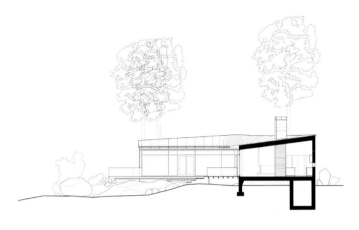

The most striking interior details are the pale ceramic tile floors and the fan-like birch wood ceiling, executed as a fine work of joinery, as was all of the built-in furniture and the kitchen cabinetwork, made mainly of walnut.

Project 1:1 Valentinswerder

Valentinswerder, Tegeler Lake, Berlin, Germany

Photographs:
Werner Hutmacher / ARTUR

In soccer, a 1:1 score is dull. In architecture, the 1:1 scale is when things get exciting, plans become facts, but architecture students can rarely test their ideas at this level. Designs start at the safe scale of 1:1000, gradually zooming in to the details, drafted at a 1:5 scale. But the first 1:1 experience often occurs after graduation, in architectural offices or construction sites in the real world, an experience known as "practice-shock".

A team of 9 Berlin University students underwent their "practice-shock" under the supervision of Per Pedersen Arch. MAA, on the small island of Valentineswerder, in Tegeler Lake, Northwest of Berlin. The students planned and constructed an extension to a summer house that belonged to two young families. This was not "Architecture without architects" but "Architecture without craftsmen".

Despite being mostly private, the island is a popular holiday venue. Several existing villas evoke a feudal past. Small summer houses and exuberant nature complete the picture. The 700 sqm plot of land is long strip by the shoreline path.

A part of the house that contained the bedrooms had been destroyed by fire. A dull prefabricated replacement was rejected, but commissioning an architect was too expensive. The owners chose to let their weekend paradise become an experiment for students. They listed their requirements: separate bedrooms for children and adults, and a toilet. They met the students for a presentation of draft proposals, returned for the presentation of the winning project, and approved it.

The front house, with the kitchen and living room, escaped the fire and guided the extension. A long raised walkway connects the two wings. To the north, level with the existing house, the walkway broadens into a terrace. On its way, the Larchwood surface unfolds a third dimension, becoming two simple houses and sheltering an intimate garden.

The "Long House" (footprint 17 sqm, volume 62 cubic meters) and the "Tall House" (footprint 14 sqm, volume 50 cubic meters.) are each family's separate space. The archetypal one-room houses are reduced to essentials: four walls, pitched roof, door, and window. Each house is divided into parent's and children's rooms: in the "Long House" a cupboard achieves this through the closing and opening of the doors; in the "Tall House" a bunk bed functions as the separation and as a horizontal cupboard. Besides the beds and the ladder, the "Tall House" is devoid of furniture.

Architects:
University of the arts, Berlin,
Faculty of Architecture
Promoter and Projectarchitect:
Per Pedersen Arch. MAA,
Ass. Professor
Projectgroup (Students):
Christian Felgendreher,
Christina Köchling, Johannes Olfs,
Stefanie Schleipen, Anna Iwanska,
Brigitte Klumps, Florian Wiedey,
Juliane Popp, Mark Niehüser
Building owner:
Nora Bierich, Toshiaki Kobayashi,
Suse Herrschmann, Johannes
Herrsmann
Plot surface:
700 sqm
Hochhaus surface:
14 sqm
Langhaus surface:
17 sqm
Start of planning:
April 2004
Start of construction:
21.07.2004
End on construction:
30.04.2005

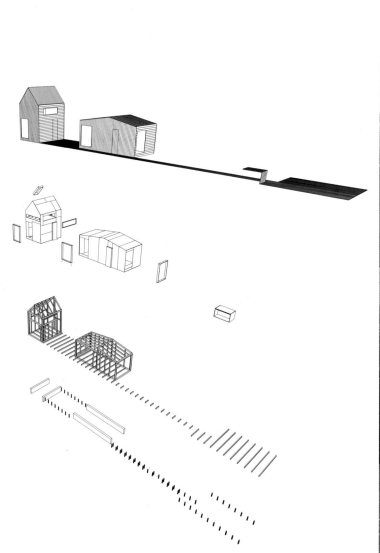

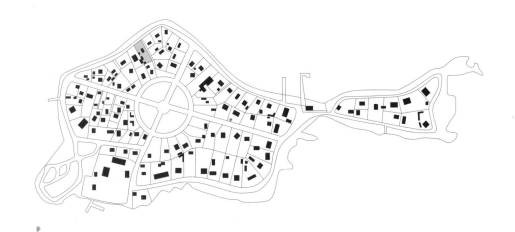

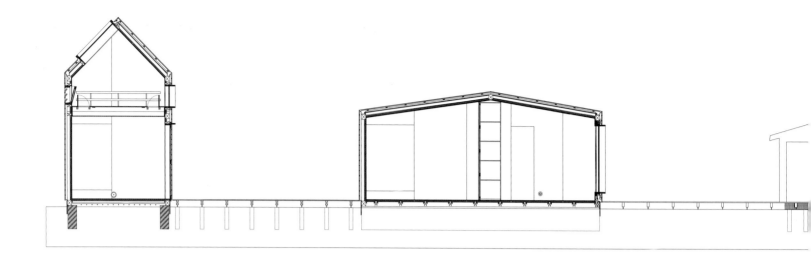

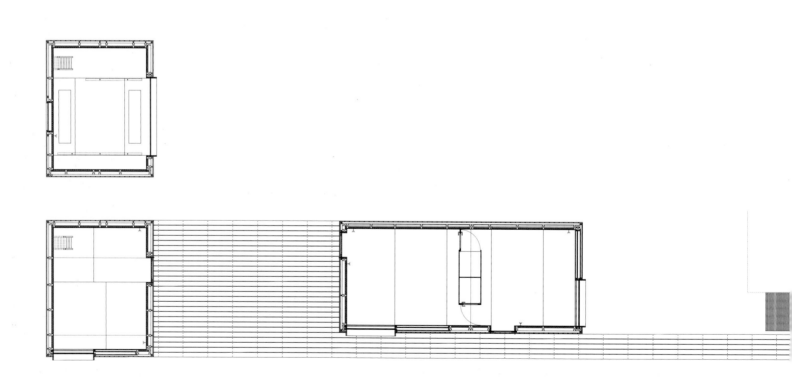

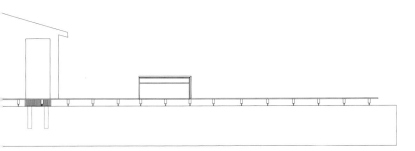

The larchwood walkway enfolds the houses, which are subtly individualized by their color: the "Long House" is dark, coldish green; the "Tall House" is fresh yellowish green. The smooth interior paneling pierces through the rough outer Larchwood cladding, to frame the windows and the door lintels.

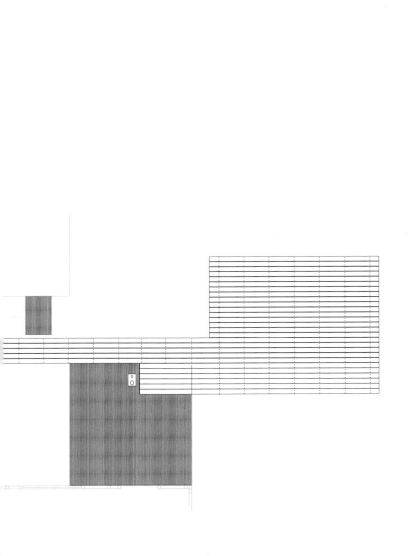

As in the entire project, the large windows are prototypes, which operate with a remarkably simple wheel mechanism. Sliding frames with mosquito netting discourage undesirable guests. The "Tall House" has two extra windows, one overlooking the lake, another facing the stars.

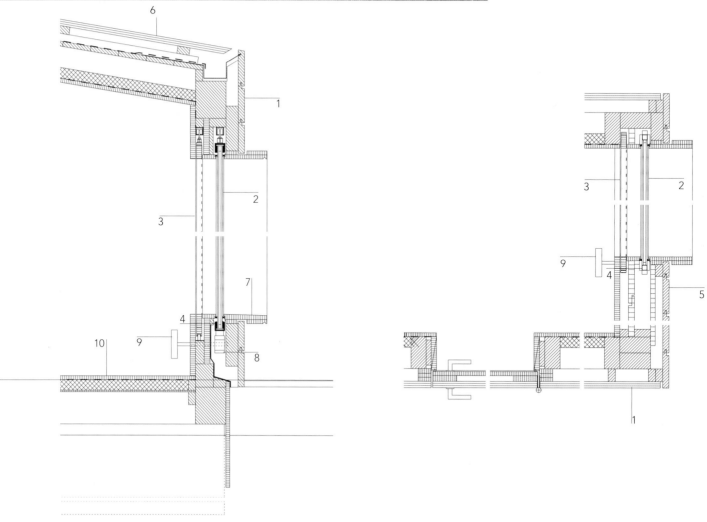

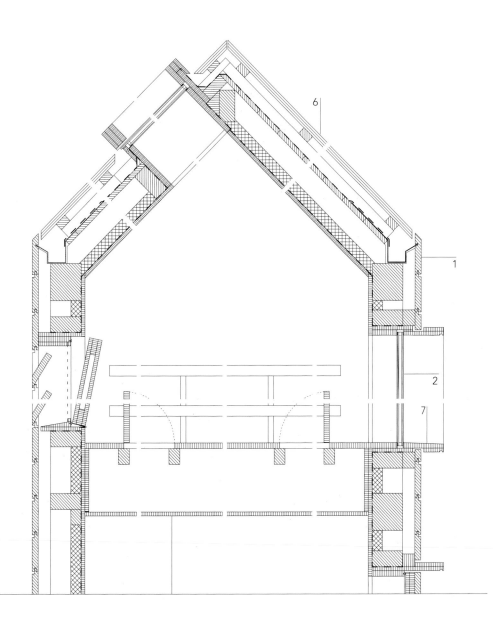

1. Tongue-and-groove matchboard, larch wood, planed, untreated 148/28 mm
Supporting member, solid wood 120/60 mm
Thermal insulation, glass wool 40 mm
Vapor barrier, birch plywood, varnished 15 mm
2. Thermopane glazing: lite 4 mm + gap between lites12 mm + lite 4 mm
3. Metal frame with fly screen, aluminum angle bar and birch plywood 15/58 mm
4. Frame: steel angle iron, U 35/40 mm, horizontal, Square steel tubing, lacquered 20/20 mm vertical
5. Tongue-and-groove matchboard, larch wood, planed, untreated 148/28 mm
Lathing 48/28 mm
OSB (oriented strand-board)-panel 22 mm
Rectangular timber 68/30 mm
OSB (oriented strand-board)-panel 22 mm
Lathing 30/30 mm,
Birch plywood, varnished 21 mm
6. Tongue-and-groove matchboard, larch wood, planed, untreated 148/28 mm
Lathing 48/28 mm
Counterlathing 48/28 mm
Bituminous sheeting, single layer 2 mm
Timber formwork, tongue-and-grooved rough boarding, spruce, 18,5/121 mm
Rafter, solid wood 120/60 mm
Thermal insulation, glass wool 40 mm
Vapor barrier, birch plywood, varnished, 15 mm
7. Birch plywood, waterproof, varnished, 15 mm
8. Dentated track, steel 30/20 mm
cogwheel and spindle, 3x embedded
9. Solid rubber wheel secured with a cotter
10. Birch plywood, varnished, 15 mm
Vapor barrier
Lathing 48/28 mm
Thermal insulation, glass wool 40 mm
Thin casing plywood 6 mm
Counterlathing 48/28 mm
Beams, solid wood 60/120 mm

Although cell-phones function here, not everyone appreciates such austere toilet arrangements and manually pumped cold water. Some may not sleep easily, aware of only a mosquito net between them and a wild boar. Those who value divorce from the urban environment will enjoy life in such purity.

Black Rubber Beach House

Dungeness, Kent, UK

Photographs:
**Chris Gascoigne / Album
/ View Pictures**

Architects:
Simon Conder Associates
Design Team:
Simon Conder and Chris Neve
Structural Engineer:
KLC Consulting Engineers
Contractor:
Charlier Construction Ltd
EPDM Sub-Contractor:
AAC Waterproofing Ltd

This project shows how the careful choice of low cost materials combined with innovatory new products can create domestic architecture of real quality at low cost.

It also proves the possibility of designing into the context of 'squatter architecture' that typifies Dungeness Beach, re-invigorating this tradition and capturing its unique spirit. Although this project started as a conversion, when the original roofing and cladding were removed, the framework was found to be virtually non-existent, so finally about 75% of the fabric was built anew.

Dungeness Beach in Kent is a classic example of 'Non Plan' and the houses along the beach have developed through improvisation and make-do. This scheme develops this tradition in a way that responds to the drama and harshness of the landscape.

The original building, the result of various changes and extensions since it was built as a fisherman's hut in the 1930s, has been stripped back to its timber frame, re-structured, extended south and east to capture the extraordinary views, and clad internally and externally in Wisa-Spruce plywood. This plywood provides all the internal finishes, including walls, floors, ceilings, doors and joinery. Externally, the walls and roof are clad in black rubber, a technical sophistication of the layers of felt and tar found on many local buildings. The bath is cantilevered out over the beach, with dramatic views to the sea.

Priority has been given to the living areas and the house only has one small bedroom. Guests are accommodated in a 1954, silver-aluminum Airstream caravan parked next to the house, a sharp contrast to the black rubber.

Innovative and sustainable, the project is the first to use EPDM (ethylene propylene diene monomer) rubber waterproofing to clad an entire building. EPDM is water resistant yet vapour permeable — withstands temperatures between -50°C and +130°C. — elongates over 400% with no degradation over time — is resistant to ozone and UV. — no fire risk — it is a natural product — individual elevations including cut-outs for doors and windows can be manufactured in the factory with vulcanized joins between roll widths.

The Wisa-Spruce plywood for the interior and external cladding of the timber frame was chosen because it comes from managed forests in Finland.

1. Deck

2. Dining / Kitchen

3. Living

4. Snug

5. Wood Burning Stove

6. Storage

7. Bedroom

8. Bathroom

9. Cantilevered Bath

10. Glazed Link

11. Floor Recessed Uplighters

12. Shed / Lobby

13. Road

14. Telegraph Pole

15. Airstream Caravan

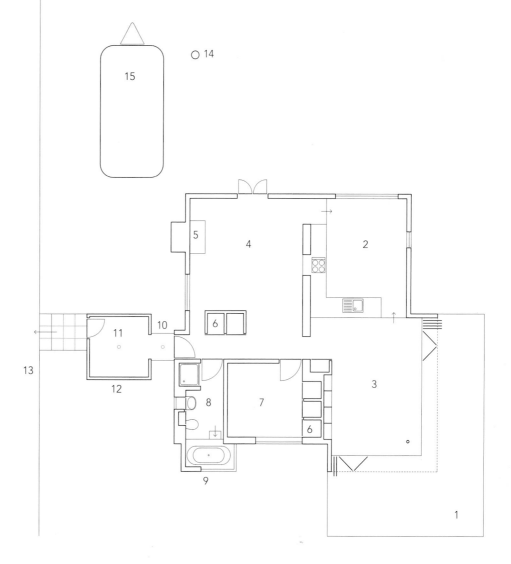

1. Pitched roof:

1.2mm EPDM black rubber membrane bonded to 18 mm WBP spruce plywood

150/50 mm C16 softwood rafters interspersed with mineral wool insulation (Tie rods at double rafters not shown: 20 mm nominal bore medium tube (BS pipework) with 26.9 mm outer diameter)

50/50 mm softwood battens interspersed with mineral wool insulation

Radiant heating film – occasional backup heating

500 Gauge polythene vapour barrier

18 mm WBP spruce plywood with clear matt intumescent decoration to achieve class 1 flame resistance rating

2. Wall:

1.2mm EPDM black rubber membrane bonded to 18 mm WBP Spruce plywood

50/50mm horizontal softwood battens interspersed with mineral wool insulation

75/50 mm vertical softwood studwork interspersed with mineral wool insulation

500 Gauge polythene vapour barrier

18 mm WBP spruce plywood with clear matt intumescent decoration to achieve class 1 flame resistance rating

3. 40/40/2 mm aluminium angle drip

4. Suspended floor:

18 mm WBP spruce plywood

1200 Gauge polythene vapour barrier

50/50 mm softwood battens interspersed with extruded polystyrene insulation

1200 Gauge polythene vapour barrier

18 mm WBP Spruce plywood

100/50 mm Softwood joists

5. New C40 concrete edge beam

6. Line of hidden lighting recess above service/ storage wall

7. 3 mm glass mirror with polished edges bonded to 18 mm WBP spruce plywood hinged panel to cabinet

8. 18 mm WBP spruce plywood perforated hinged panel screening window – 20 mm Ø holes drilled in a 50 mm grid

9. 1700/750/430 mm double ended white enamelled steel bath

10. 2 × 18 mm WBP spruce plywood cantilevered bath step

11. 70/70/6 mm galvanised RSA side panel frame to cantilevered bath cubicle with 50/5 mm galvanised MS flat diagonal

12. 70/70/4 mm galvanised SHS principle frame to cantilevered bath cubicle

13. 60.3/4 mm galvanised CHS with 60/10 mm galvanised MS flat welded to each end for bolted connections (Diagonal bracing is duplicated within wall between bathroom and bedroom)

14. C40 concrete counterweight to cantilevered bath cubicle

Section through cantilevered bath cubicle

1. Flat roof:

1.2 mm EPDM black rubber membrane bonded to 18mm WBP Spruce plywood

150/50 mm C16 softwood joists interspersed with mineral wool insulation

50/50 mm softwood battens interspersed with mineral wool insulation

Radiant heating film – occasional backup heating

500 gauge polythene vapour barrier

18 mm WBP spruce plywood with clear matt intumescent decoration to achieve class 1 flame resistance rating

2. Canopy:

1.2mm EPDM black rubber membrane bonded to 12 + 18 mm WBP spruce plywood

100/50 mm galvanised PFC frame sandwiching 80/75mm C24 softwood to take folding sliding glazed door system head track

500 gauge polythene vapour barrier

18 mm WBP Spruce plywood with clear matt intumescent decoration to achieve class 1 flame resistance rating

3. Folding sliding bottom running double-glazed door system with 4/20/4 mm clear toughened sealed units – inner pane Pilkington K

4. Solid floor:

18mm WBP spruce plywood

1200 gauge polythene vapour barrier

50/50mm softwood battens interspersed with extruded polystyrene insulation

1200 gauge polythene vapour barrier

5. Original concrete raft

6. New C40 concrete with Fibrin X-T and plasticiser

7. 18 mm WBP spruce plywood kitchen units

8. 18 mm WBP spruce plywood raised service floor – aiding plumbing runs

9. 18 mm WBP spruce plywood hinged panel with cable notch to hidden electrical sockets

10. 90/25 mm PAR hardwood decking with 10mm gaps set at 20 mm below internal floor level

11. 100/50 mm galvanised PFC side panel frame to canopy

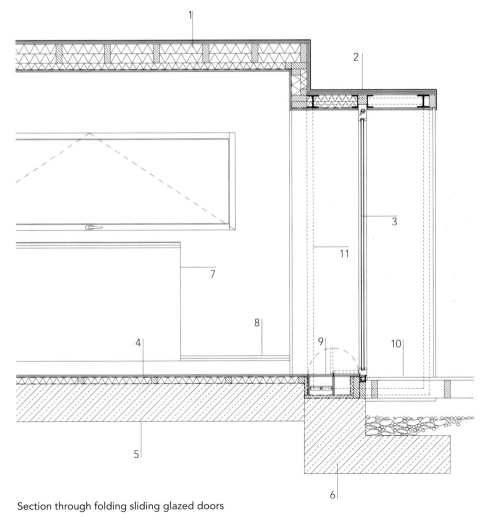

Section through folding sliding glazed doors

Besonias - Almeida -Kruk

Casa Mar Azul

Mar Azul, Buenos Aires, Argentina

Photographs:
Mariana Rapaport

Mar Azul is a seaside town situated 400 km (250 miles) south of Buenos Aires, with an extensive beach of virgin sand dunes and a dense conifer forest. The owners, members of the architectural studio and regular visitors to the area, chose this splendid forest backdrop especially, to build this small summer house.

The environmental and scenic characteristics of the site, its particular use and the absence of a client to set premises for the project allowed the architects to view this construction as a possibility to experiment, both in terms of function and aesthetic-constructive solutions.

The search for alternatives had just three limitations: a minimal impact on the landscape, a low budget, and a building that would need almost zero maintenance. With these premises in mind, it was decided to build the house as a prism of minimum height, defined by an envelope of exposed concrete, which harmonizes in texture and color with the forest, and by large window panes, which reflect the surroundings and allow the house to integrate completely with its setting. The complementary functions (spare bathroom, water tank and deposit) are housed in a vertical, wooden prism, hidden among the trees.

The simple volume that accommodates the main functions was divided into two very different areas: one totally glazed, surrounded by a wide, wooden terrace, designed for reunions and totally integrated with the forest, and the other more protected, with more modest openings and used for the bedrooms, the bathroom and a space for cooking. The house has no official entranceway: it can be accessed via the glazed section, through sliding doors located on two of the facades. This way of entering, together with the spatial vagueness of the lounge area, allows for widely diverse uses. Two metal sliding doors can be shut, when required, separating this area from the other rooms.

Being regular visitors to the forest, the architects understood the need for ensuring a generous entry of light. To reinforce the panes of glass, an L-shaped light entry point was incorporated into the center of the floor plan, coinciding with two sides of the bathroom. The effect, in the bathroom and lounge area alike, is lighting that changes throughout the course of the day. The artificial lighting was aimed at highlighting the indistinctness of the house's main area, with lamps that can be altered in both direction and intensity.

Architects:
María Victoria Besonías, Guillermo de Almeida, Luciano Kruk.
Collaborator:
Diego Grosso
Plot surface:
470 m²
Building surface:
75 m²
Cost:
800 pesos/m²
Construction year:
2004
Construction time:
6 months

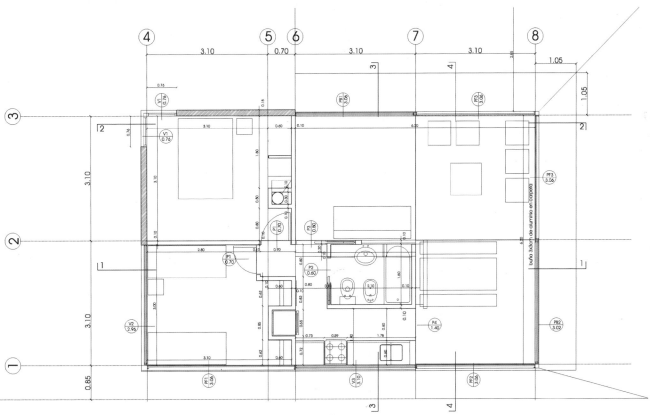

105

The microclimate of this seaside forest and the house's frequent use in mild or warm seasons, permitted a low-cost constructive solution, which could be quickly realized, based on an envelope of exposed concrete with no complements needed to improve the thermal insulation. Furthermore, the expressive qualities of exposed concrete, together with its properties of resistance and impermeability, made any surface finish unnecessary.

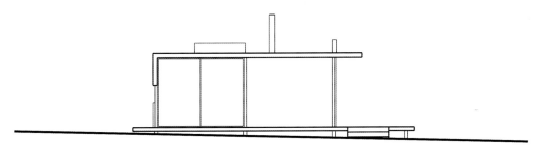

Northeast elevation

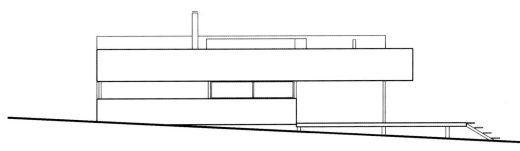

Southeast elevation

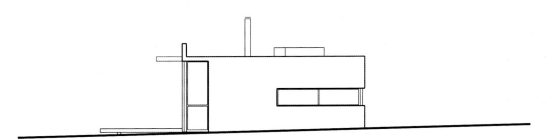

Southwest elevation

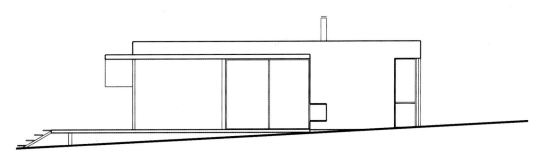

Northwest elevation

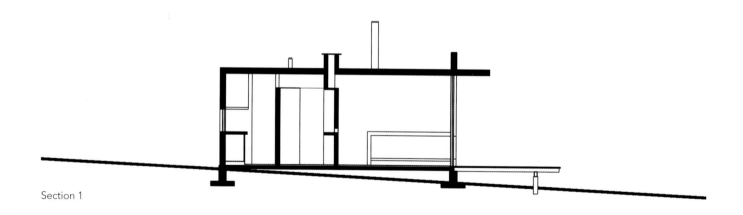

Section 1

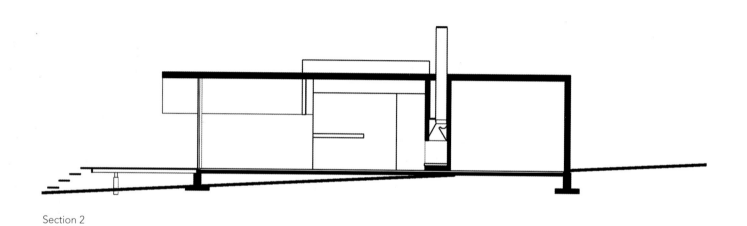

Section 2

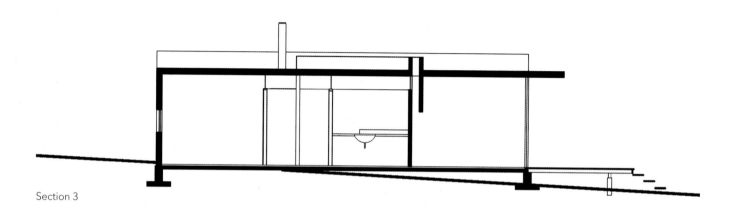

Section 3

The furniture, especially designed for this house, was made from Canadian pine salvaged from packaging boxes for engines.

The control of the light and exterior visuals was resolved through *black out* curtains in the bedrooms and *boile* curtains in the glazed section.

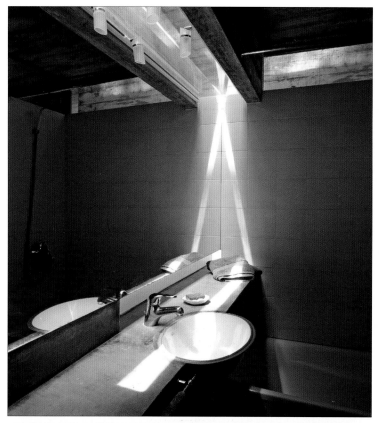

1. Supplementary block
2. Galvanized sheet metal No. 18
3. Batten fixture block
4. Rafters 2' x 4'
5. Columns 0.12 x 0.12
6. Planks 1.80 x 0.10 x ½'
7. Batten 2' x 2'
8. 2'x 4' diagonal ties
9. Insert columns 0.12 x 0.12
10. Rafters 2' x 6'
11. Boarding ½'
12. Roof frame diam. 6 mm C/20 mm
13. Supplementary strips
14. Rafter 2'x 4' (permanent formwork)
15. Roof frame diam. 6 mm (quantity. 3 bars)
16. Column section painted with coal tar
17. Reinforced concrete pile
18. Finishing angle
19. Nail with hermetic head
20. Folded sheet metal
21. Polycarbonate

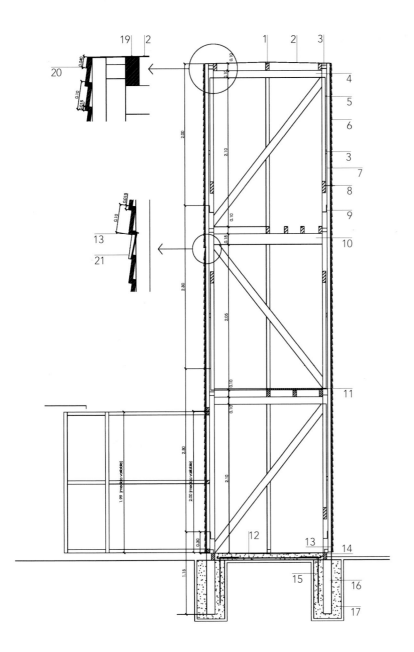

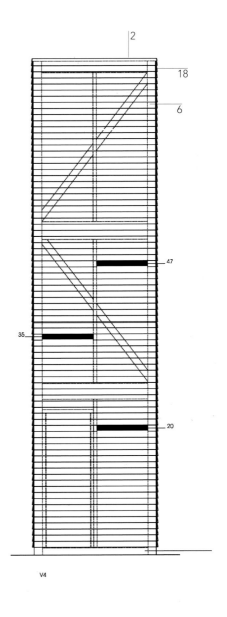

V4

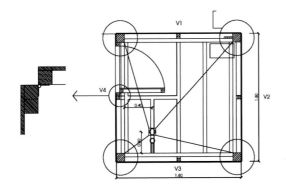

Eggleston | Farkas Architects

Methow Cabin

Winthrop, Washington, USA

Photographs:
Jim Van Gundy

Architects:
Eggleston / Farkas Architects

Chosen "House of the Month" by Architectural Record in October 2003, it also earned the Honor Award in the 2002 AIA Northwest and Pacific Region Design Awards and a Citation Award at the AIA Seattle Honor Awards for Washington Architecture. The juror's comments: "Here the architects start all over with the Northwest vernacular, going back to the roots with a simple, distilled language, in a beautifully stripped-down version, a true emerging voice, a lone rider on the prairie."

The Methow Cabin stands in a sparse meadow adjacent to a network of cross-country skiing trails along the floor of the valley. The program was to create a small retreat, serving as a base for cross-country skiing and mountain biking excursions. The owners wished to accommodate groups of 6 to 8 people with a communal area for gathering and dining.

The building has been placed in alignment with the valley, opening at the ends to focus on the views up and down the valley. The service zone shields the living spaces from the road. A slot window - positioned for seated viewing - frames skiers as they glide by.

The structure consists of Glulam beams with wood decking to span the gap between a wood framed fin wall and the utility zone. The exterior cedar siding is continued through the living spaces to create a continuum of interior and exterior space. Steel details were designed for ease of fabrication by local agricultural welders.

The shed roof echoes the slope of the hills beyond, while allowing snow to slide off easily. There are no roof penetrations, and the simple form eliminates ridges and valleys that would be susceptible to leaks. The shed creates both a protected entry porch at the low end and a sleeping loft at the high end. Accessed from the side, the entry stair remains snow-free even as snow avalanches dramatically off the end.

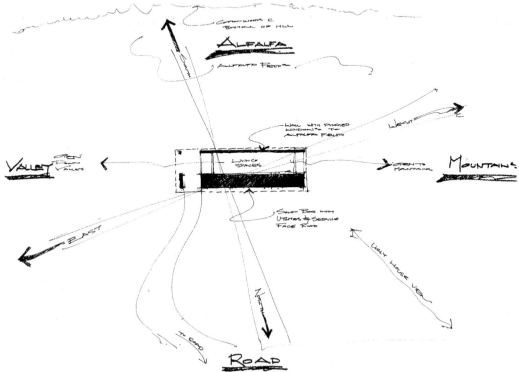

The foundation was required to extend 4' below grade, to lie below the frost line. By using 8' vertical forms, a single pour provided sufficient depth while raising the wood structure 4' above grade to protect it from snowdrifts. Sufficient ceiling height was created for the downstairs bunkroom, with a protected at-grade window below the deck. Excavation spoils were used to form a mound for access to the entry porch.

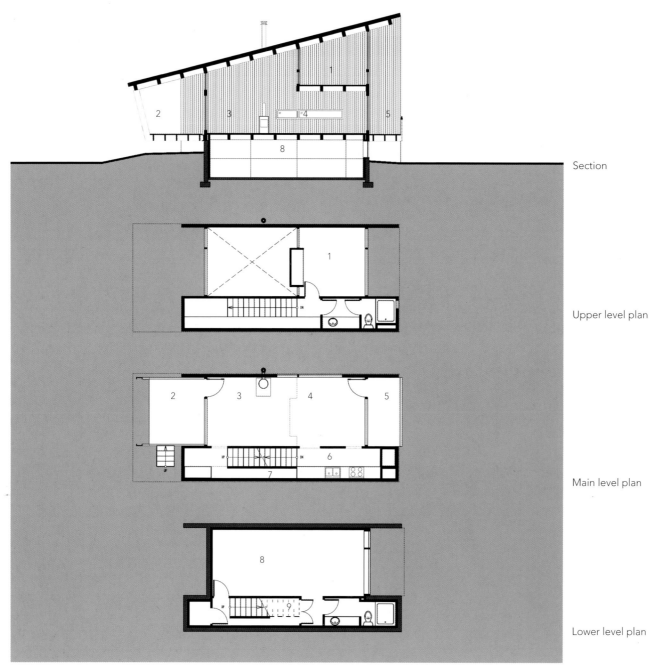

Section

Upper level plan

Main level plan

Lower level plan

1. Sleeping loft
2. Porch
3. Living
4. Dining
5. Deck

6. Kitchen
7. Ski storage
8. Bunk room
9. Mechanical

120

Eggleston | Farkas Architects

Port Hadlock Cabin

Port Hadlock, Washington, USA

Photographs:
Jim Van Gundy

Architects:
Eggleston | Farkas Architects

The parcel occupies a projection of the shoreline overlooking a wetland & marina to the north-east, an island to the north, and a tidal cove to the west. Site constraints include a shared access road, a stream, a steep bluff, the shoreline, the wetland, and an abandoned logging debris burn-pit.

The program involved the creation of a vacation cabin with separate zones for the owners and their guests, but with a shared gathering space. The owners' involvement in a land conservation organization explain their consequent desire to keep impact to the site under strict control and to restore the unbuilt parts of the plot to their natural state.

The solution decided on was to build the cabin over the burn pit itself, as the way to avoid impacting the more sensitive parts of the land, while rectifying the most damaged. The debris from the burn pit was removed to reach solid bearing. Eight-foot tall foundations were poured, creating an elevated platform for the main living spaces with space for boat storage below. The house has been oriented to take advantage of the different views from within the various spaces. The main wing faces the marina and wetlands, while the guest wing faces the cove. A large screen porch at the knuckle is a communal gathering place that offers panoramic views. The 'L' shape also creates an outdoor space that is sheltered from the prevailing winds and is open to the morning sun. Architectural Record chose it as the house of the month in October 2003.

Expressing the flow of water on the site, a pair of corrugated metal shed roofs provide a covered walkway at the access area between the structures. Rainwater is collected by a shared gutter and allowed to drop into a basin; from there it is redistributed to its natural destination – the stream, the wetlands, and Puget Sound.

The parcel occupies a projection of the shoreline overlooking a wetland & marina to the northeast, an island to the north, and a tidal cove to the west. Site constraints include a shared access road, a stream, a steep bluff, the shoreline, the wetland, and an abandoned logging debris burn-pit.

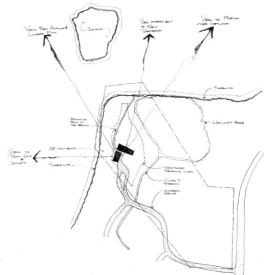

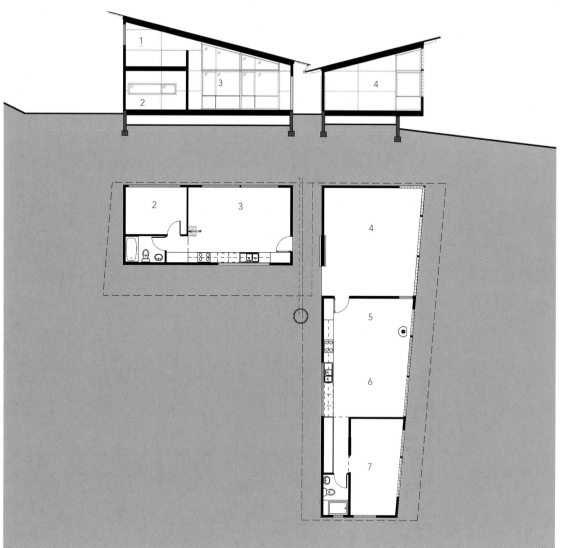

1. Loft
2. Bedroom
3. Rec room
4. Screen porch
5. Living
6. Dining
7. Bedroom

The house has been oriented to take advantage of the different views from within the various spaces. The main wing faces the marina and wetlands, while the guest wing faces the cove. A large screen porch at the knuckle is a communal gathering place that offers panoramic views.

Bruno Keller

Dock and Workshop at Caslano

Caslano, Lugano, Switzerland

Photographs:
Lorenzo Mussi

Architect:
Bruno Keller
Civil engineer:
Andrea Pedrazzini
Collaborators:
Dragos Dordea, Simona Dirvariu,
Martino Keller
Clients:
Dilva and Mario Veragouth

The new construction was designed to replace a precarious existing structure, on the shore of Lake Lugano. The new bearing structure consists of five structural frames made of steel box-girders, one end of which is anchored in the strong concrete wall along the lakeside; on the landward side, the frames are anchored in the contention wall that sustains the access road.

The new infrastructure of the dry dock cantilevers over the water, suspended on the supports provided by the steel structure: the result is a hinged cover or deck that provides the accessory for raising boats of a reasonable size. Next to it are two fully enclosed cubicles, which contain the various maintenance and service facilities.

An opening through the hinged deck leads to the landing jetty, reached by means of a hinged stairway, at an angle which adapts automatically to the level of the lake at any given time.

The hinged deck and the two cubicles constitute a rectangular geometrical composition, made entirely of fir wood, glass enclosed openings with aluminum carpentry, and heavy duty marine plywood framing.

The two cubicles, the interior dimensions of which are 9.5 feet wide, 12.14 feet long and 7.41 feet high, are potentially usable as a makeshift apartment. To provide for such a use, a compact bathroom and kitchen have been included.

The bathroom has the basic necessary accessories of a shower, a washbasin and a toilet. These items are reduced to a simple composition of complementary geometrical forms, clad in sheets of synthetic veneer, enhancing a rational use of the little space available.

Work on the outside walls has been reduced to the minimum; to secure the shoreline, a solid concrete dam has been constructed, with a line of built-in steps leading down to the water.

The only added element of furniture is a bas-relief composition of polychrome wooden tiles, installed along the sustaining wall under the access road, created by the client to conceal a suspended tank.

The result embodies an attempt to unify, as much as possible, the specific characteristics of the site and the client's requirements, by means of a straightforward and natural use of materials, regarding the steel frame support structure, and the best distribution and use of the location's unique natural light.

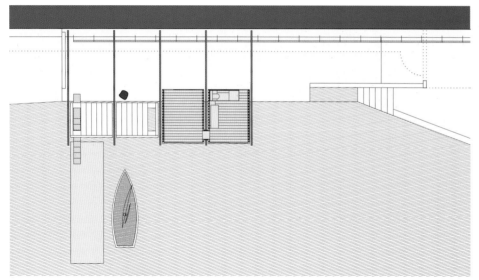

The hinged deck and the two cubicles constitute a rectangular geometrical composition, made entirely of fir wood, glass enclosed openings with aluminum carpentry, and heavy duty marine plywood framing.

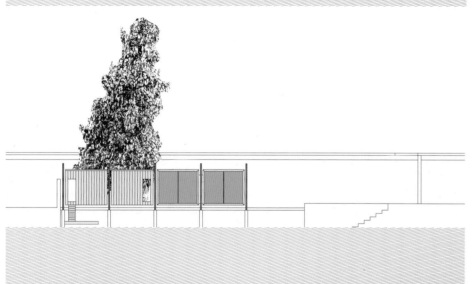

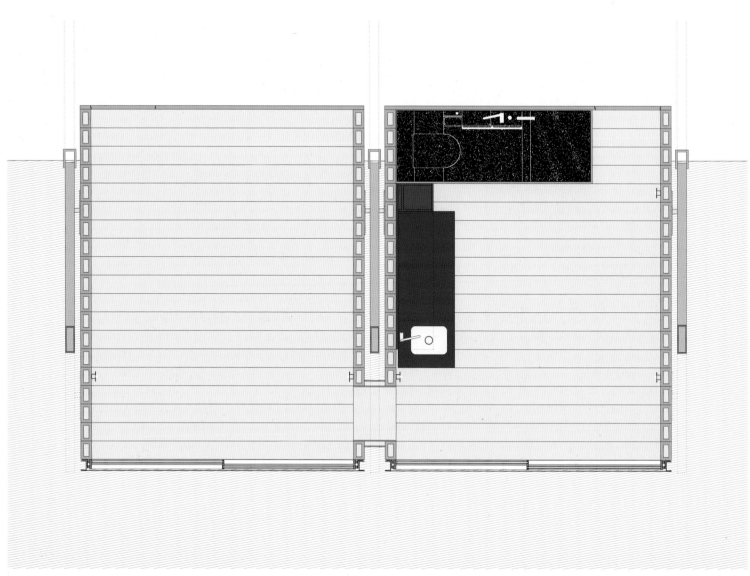

Woodland Cabin

Ronse, Belgium

Photographs:
Kristien Daem

Architects:
Paul Robbrecht & Hilde Daem
Assistant:
Catherine Fierens
Landscape architect:
Herman Seghers

For many, the proverbial hut in the woods is a recurrent dream, an object of desire that most people treasure among their childhood memories, but few can make serious plans to materialize.
An art and design collector who lives in the hills in southern Flanders, Belgium, purchased a piece of unspoiled, densely wooded land near his home. He then commissioned architects Paul Robbrecht and Hilde Daem, together with landscape architect Herman Seghers, to create a use for this property without affecting the wonder of its untouched natural condition. Wooden planks were used to create winding woodland paths, which wander through the environment, circumventing obstacles, and occasionally rising or descending a few steps to overcome a slope or avoid a group of trees. These interventions are not intended to do more than leave a trace in an environment which remains essentially unchanged. The project seeks a contact with nature that preserves its original state, unshaped by man. The course of the path follows the topography of the land, which also inspired the location of the hut; near the bottom of the dell, where the land lies lowest, and a seasonal pond appears when water gathers there every springtime and autumn.

Standing on a platform built above a stream, the cabin serves as a rudimentary lodging, for the enjoyment of silence, birds, animals and plants. The small building consist of two circular spaces, one of which contains little more than a bed; the other encloses a limited seating area with a couple of chairs, a wood stove and a stack of wood. So far, all other household activities, such as washing and cooking, take place in the open air.

The walls around this two-lobed floor plan are made of stacked wooden blocks joined with dowel pegs. The roof consists of a radial pattern of beams and boards covered with blocks of peat. The result integrates harmoniously with the environment, yet states its alien individual presence. The object evokes what the architects claim as their source of inspiration, scenes out of 'Nanouk of the North', a black and white documentary from 1920, or the stone huts built by the inhabitants of the Alpujarra mountains in southern Spain, or a number of other basic rural structures leading back to the earliest forms of shelter. In a poetical way, the hut in Flanders refers to all archetypical constructions.

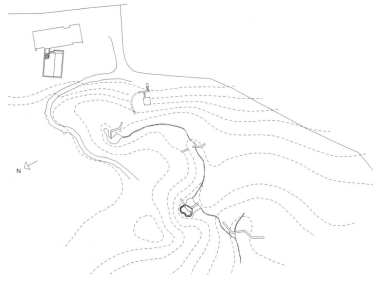

Wooden planks were used to create winding woodland paths, which wander through the environment, circumventing obstacles, and occasionally rising or descending a few steps to overcome a slope or avoid a group of trees.
The course of the path follows the topography of the land, which also inspired the location of the hut: near the bottom of the dell, where the land lies lowest, and a seasonal pond appears every springtime and autumn, when water gathers there.

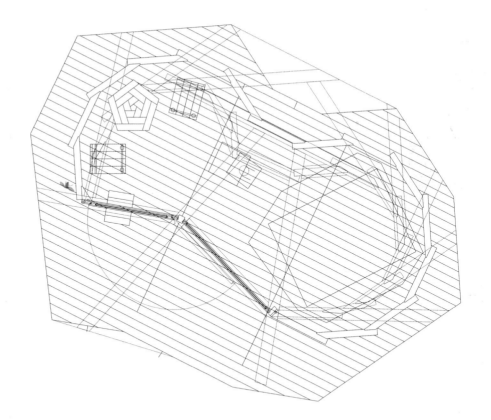

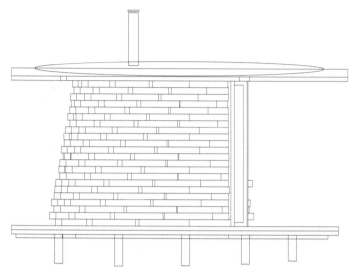

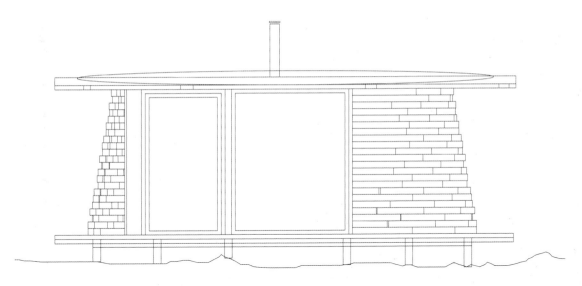

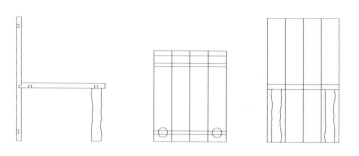

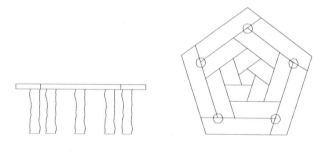

Eduardo Martín Martín

House in Granada

Vega de Granada, Spain

La Vega de Granada is a protected rural area on the outskirts of the city with wide open views that end with the snowy peaks of the Sierra Nevada. Broken up by tall poplars and small isolated buildings, the landscape changes with the seasons.

This small house was built on the ruins of an old shed made out of black poplar wood. The authorities ruled that its volume should be the same as the original shed. Its casing is a box made out of planks treated with nothing more than pesticide protection so that they acquire the patina that usually comes with time, and their colouring is in harmony with the environment. There are similar farm buildings scattered all over the area, like for example tobacco driers where this material has been traditionally used. This is an architectural box built out of wood in a rectangular shape, using timber from specific harvesting.

It shares a plot of land with two other houses. An effort has been made to preserve the trees on the land, old enough to look like sculptures in the surrounding countryside. It is situated at a tangent in its plot, quite close to the back of another rural building.

A far cry from the usual demands for domestic housing this one is kept to a minimum, at 75 square metres. Being isolated makes it possible to do away with entrance hall or corridors, so the given space is all used for interconnecting living rooms or storage. The layout is structured into three modular areas on 4.25 metres axes. The central module contains the sitting room, with doors designed as panels as if they are a continuation of the floor. These panels are used to create intimate spaces (for reading, being quiet.). Warm light is a feature, being overhead but diffused through the elm trees, combining well with the cold clear light from the picture window.

On either side of the living room are two bedrooms at the front, and the kitchen-dining room and bathroom at the rear. A cupboard runs along the longitudinal axis of the house providing storage space for clothes, kitchen fixtures, and utility room: With the exception of one window all the openings are doors which give direct access to the outside from the different rooms.

The southern side is closed in so as not to be overlooked by the neighbouring house. Two materials, wood and coloured metal, make up the outer layer of the house and are repeated on the inside, even in the fixed furniture. This home is totally open to the countryside so there is no sense of claustrophobia despite its small size. When the doors are folded back the house opens up and lets the outdoor landscape in.

Photographs:
**Eugeni Pons,
Vicente del Amo**

Architects:
**Eduardo Martín Martín, Luis Javier
Martín Martín, martín & martín
arquitectos**
Project manager:
**Eduardo Martín Martín, Luis Javier
Martín Martín**
Constructor:
Gabriel Vallejo S.L.
Client:
**Eduardo Martín Martín,
Olimpia Gómez Rivero**
Surface:
**84.5 m² (house),
52.8 m² (terrace)**

▲Vicente del Amo

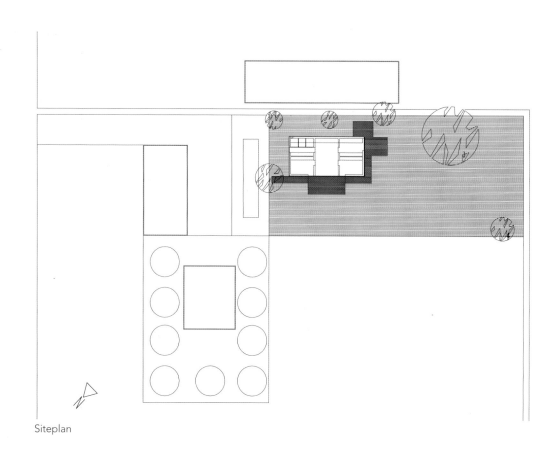

Siteplan

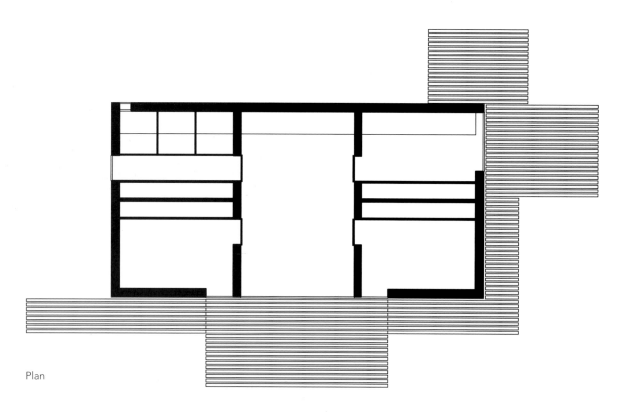

Plan

Wooden decking at varying levels marks the transition between the building and the countryside.

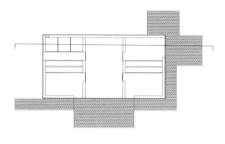

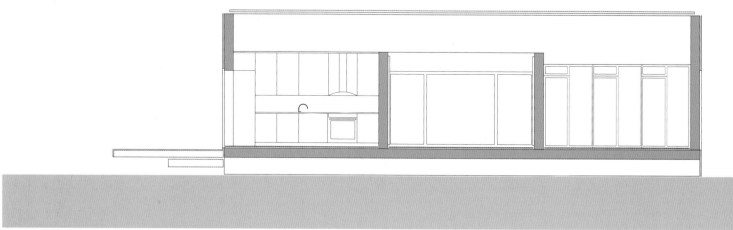

Longitudinal section

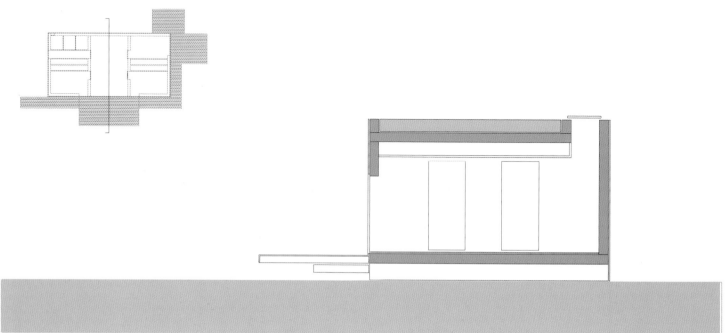

Cross section

▲Eugeni Pons

Eugeni Pons ▲

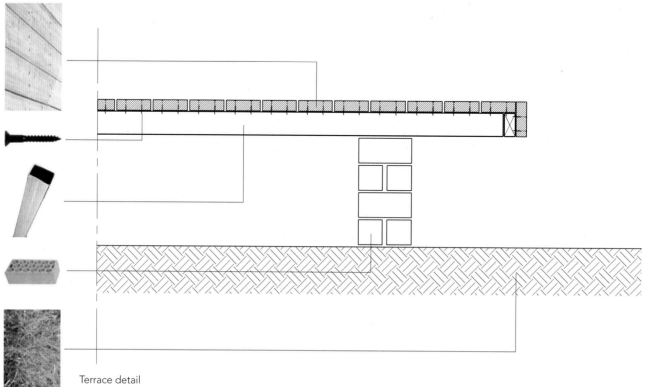

Terrace detail

▲ Eugeni Pons

Interior doors detail

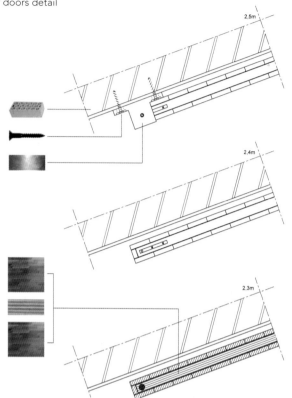

2,5m

2,4m

2.3m

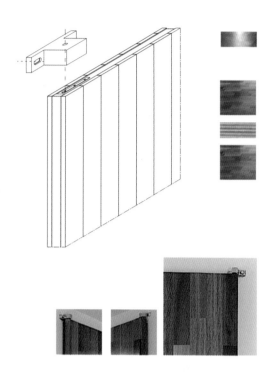

Vicente del Amo ▲   ▲Vicente del Amo

Detail of wall between bathroom and hall

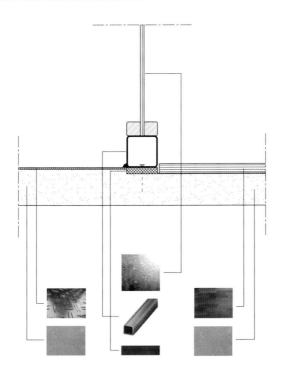

Detail of exterior bathroom wall

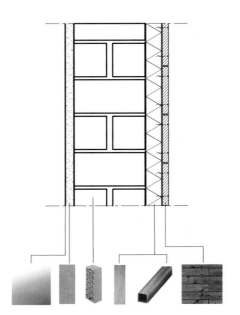

▲Vicente del Amo

▲Vicente del Amo

The central module contains the sitting room, with doors designed as panels as if they are a continuation of the floor. On either side of the living room are two bedrooms at the front, and the kitchen-dining room and bathroom at the rear.

▲Vicente del Amo

Hemmi Fayet Architekten

Vacation House at Zinal

Zinal Switzerland

Photographs:
Hannes Henz

Architects Hemmi and Fayet have authored an unusual holiday home over the village of Zinal in Switzerland. The local style is made reference to, albeit in the architect's unobtrusive personal language devoid of badly integrated regional accents. "We want to understand what matters to our clients. It is not a question of materializing a current aesthetic but of discovering a common language. All mediums are good enough for us", says Serge Fayet. In order to find the best placement for the building in the landscape, architects Petra Hemmi and Serge Fayet, together with the client, laid out the footprint of the building with stones. At a later stage, they stretched out pieces of cloth over the lines of stones, to show the inner distribution. Fayet calls this a real luxury, because an architect's timetable rarely allows for such methods. As Zinal is too far from Zurich to drive back in the same day, they stayed overnight. "It is amazing to work without a model, to take the methods learned at the ETH in Zurich and translate them to a 1:1 scale. Usually the architect comes to the site, determines the points of the compass and uses this information to develop his design. "It is something quite different to be somewhere and study the light throughout the day". The two designers know what they are talking about, having held long term assistant posts at ETH in Zurich, where they and their students translated design theories into reality. "For us, the client's interests come first. We don't wish to make architecture the most important aspect of which is our own handwriting". At the earliest stage of design, designated as "zero", the question is all about getting to know each other, seeking a common basis and discovering if it will be possible to work together. The clients gather everything they like, pictures out of decoration magazines, drawings, patterns, materials and more. One of the concepts this team claims as fundamental in their work is that color and space are interrelated.

Architects:
Hemmi Fayet Architekten
Structure engineer:
Makiol und Wiederkehr,
Beinwil am See
Timber construction:
Gebr. Wilk AG, Niederlenz
Furniture:
Lenzlinger Söhne AG, Uster
Plot surface:
650 sqm
Building surface:
152 sqm
Cost:
765.000 CHF

The location is a 650 sqm plot of the land. Each floor in the building has a usable floor space of 152 sqm. The building's entire inner volume totals 735 cubic meters, securely based on a plinth of reinforced concrete.

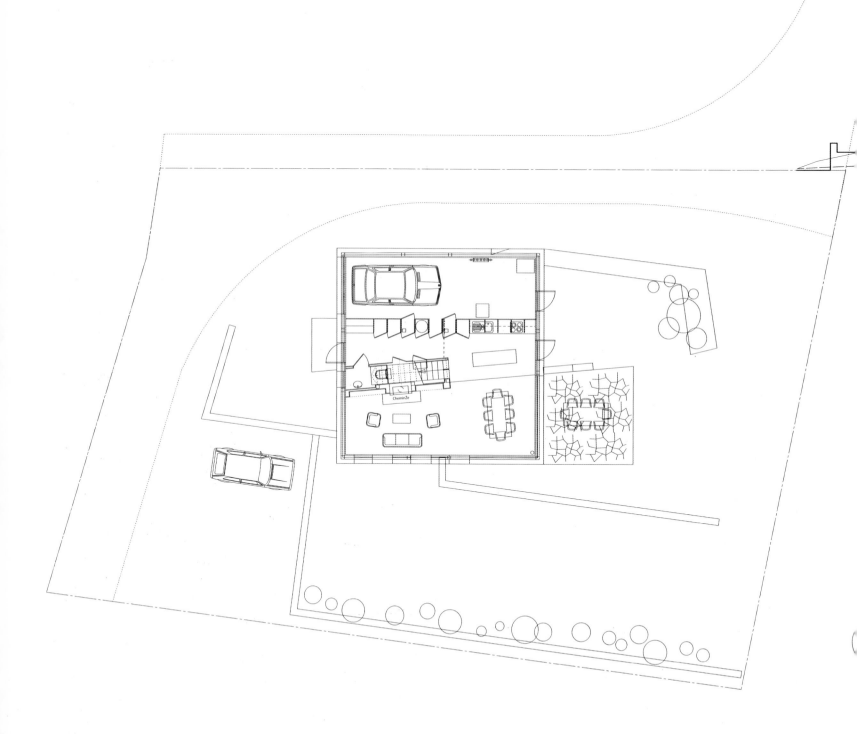

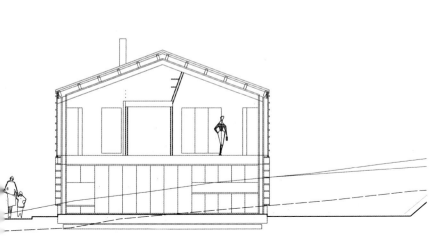

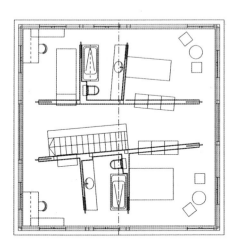

The exterior cladding consists of three-layered Douglas-fir plywood, rough-finished, treated with a protective varnish over a base-coat of natural oils. The walls of the ground-floor are made of wood with exterior shelving to contain the firewood. The walls of the upper floor are double layered wood planking with an aerated insulation layer inside.

All the rooms in the upper floor are connected, like a suite, by a central common space, which also connects them to the floor below.

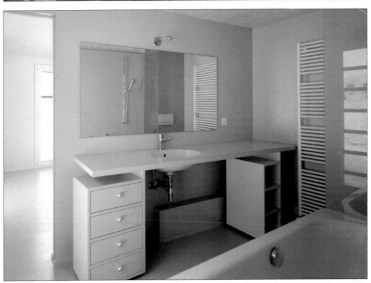

Y-Hutte

East Japan

Widely acclaimed Japanese architect Kengo Kuma has described his approach to designing this home in the midst of nature in seemingly simple terms: "I reflected upon how a hut in a forest should be." Considering how important the thinking process prior to design is for him, this statement is particularly meaningful. In his work he aims to produce buildings that are "some kind of frame of nature" enabling a deeper, more intimate experience of nature, even when they are in the middle of an intense city. The environment in this project is a key to its resolution. Kengo Kuma considered drawing a quadrilateral plan on a perpendicular Cartesian coordinate system but rejected it as it would restrict the direction and would be too artificial and constructive in the natural forest. As he says himself "I am more interested in an architecture that is 'close to nature'." The result was that he dreamt up a form structured by resting three panels on each other to produce a triangular pyramid and cutting its corners. A large single-space is created by the three panels.

The panels, functioning as both roof and wall, are held by wooden ribs at 300mm pitch. These ribs give an effect of diffusing light just like the branches and leaves of a tree. The slanted panels meet together in a tree-like manner, giving an impression of the top branches of trees tied together. This effect is the reason why Frank Lloyd Wright and Buckminster Fuller preferred triangular to rectangular form for its quality of resembling nature. The plan becomes a hexagon, and when each edge is given different elements -dining table and chairs, fire place, piano, kitchen counter, bed, writing table - the elements are adjoined in obtuse angles and dispersed in the space creating a loosely partitioned room.

An Ondor-type (Korean floor heater) floor heating system was installed. Hot air is sent under the space between the doubled-floor, and vented through the slit opened near the window to prevent condensation.

In summer, air conditioning is limited to ventilation as the climate is cool. The tilted panels and high ceiling enable ventilation through natural gravity. In addition, the sky lights are positioned in such a way that they correspond to the prevailing wind which cools and therefore creates effective ventilation.

Photographs:
Edmund Sumner / Album / View Pictures

Architects:
Kengo Kuma & Associates
Principal in charge:
Kengo Kuma
Project team:
Masamichi Hirabayashi, Taiko Kasai
Structural engineer:
Structural Design Office Ejiri
Mechanical engineer:
P.T Mourima & Associates, Ltd
General contractor:
Dai'ichi Kensetsu Ltd
Site area:
1,127.8 sqm
Built area:
73.37 sqm
Total floor area:
90.51 sqm

This hut, designed through the investigation of the form, "close to nature", somehow resembles the "Primitive Hut" described by Laugier in the eighteenth century, and to ancient pit dwellings. Kengo Kuma, known for his desire to recover the tradition of Japanese architecture and to reinterpret it for the 21st century, brings together historical architectural references and his own aims in this ingenious forest hut.

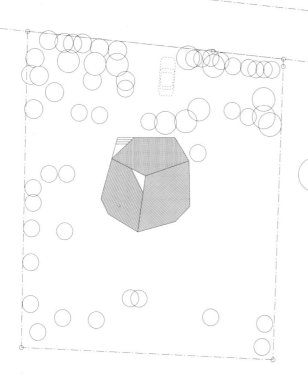

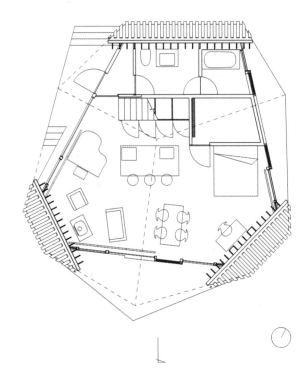

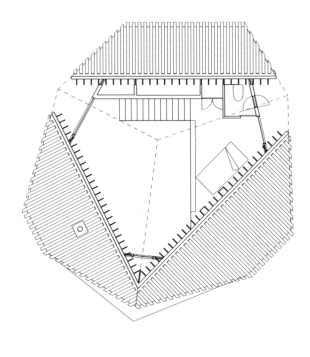

Ground floor plan

First floor plan

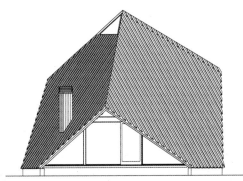

South elevation

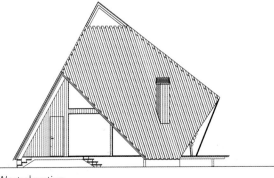

West elevation

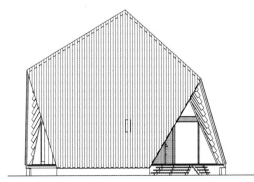

North elevation

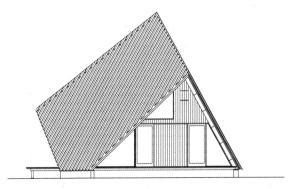

East elevation

171

The plan becomes a hexagon, and when each edge is given different elements -dining table and chairs, fire place, piano, kitchen counter, bed, writing table - the elements are adjoined in obtuse angles and dispersed in the space creating a loosely partitioned room.

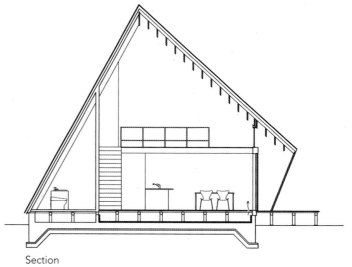

Section

Ullmayer & Sylvester Architects

The Summerhouse

London, UK

Photographs:
Kilian O'Sullivan / Album / View Pictures

Architects:
Ullmayer & Sylvester Architects
Structural engineer:
BTA Structural Design
Surface:
35 sqm
Cost:
35.000 £
Construction time:
7 weeks

When Ullmayer and Sylvester Architects were commissioned to design the summerhouse, they took it as an opportunity to work on a fairly unprecedented building type - somewhere between an Eames pavilion and a south coast caravan, neither an extension nor a garden shed, and located in a tricky context. Its 35.000 £ budget was a challenging squeeze, which was met in 7 weeks.

The clients, a Hackney-based family of four, wanted a seasonal hideaway, as the children grow, and more play space is needed. The new space should serve as a painter's studio, for the father to paint away from the children. The boys should gain an occasional sleep-over in summer. The mother, a talented gardener, needed a tool shed. The structure's overall dimensions must accommodate the family's obsession with table tennis. Developing the somewhat neglected rear of their garden became an alternative to moving into a larger property.

Design started from a box that was gradually moulded fit its environment. The building was kinked to form an intimate enclosure at the rear, squeezed where plants needed priority, and fanned out where the inside wanted to be generous. Openings were formed in response to the rhythm of the tree trunks, the roof was folded like a butterfly. It was found that a softwood and birch ply structure, internally fully exposed, achieved these moves with ease. This structure would rest on a steel frame, resting in turn upon shallow concrete pads, to avoid damaging the roots of the trees.

The tight budget imposed a traditional timber frame construction, but the details have received the utmost attention, with planed smooth surfaces and controlled, pristine joints that are fully revealed in the interior, skillfully carried out by the carpenters. From the back of its elongated Victorian garden, the resulting structure screens out the urban setting, while toying with baroque ideas of illusion, distortion, and camouflage, capturing nature to create a surprisingly rigorous contemporary building that measures 35 sqm plus the decks.

The thin skin that clads the exterior affords the required weather protection. Moreover, these surfaces are intended to underline the presence of the garden, framing the seasons. An 8 meter long mirror reflects the vegetation, defying the solidity and proximity of the wall it is mounted on. Semi-transparent striped polycarbonate plays with the shadows of the leaves, shimmering above.

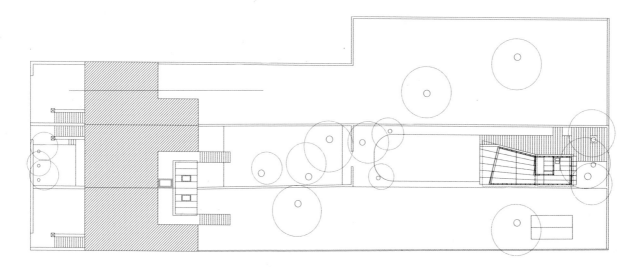

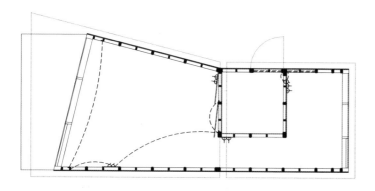
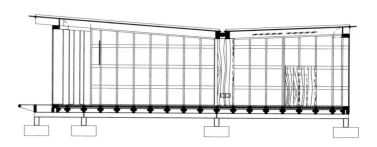

From the back of its elongated Victorian garden, the resulting structure screens out the urban setting, while toying with baroque ideas of illusion, distortion, and camouflage, capturing nature to create a surprisingly rigorous contemporary building.

The tight budget imposed a traditional timber frame construction, but the details have received the utmost attention, with planed smooth surfaces and controlled, pristine joints that are fully revealed in the interior, skillfully carried out by the carpenters.

Felipe Assadi

Buzeta House

Maitencillo, Puchuncaví, Chile

Photographs:
Guy Wenborne

Architect:
Felipe Assadi
Civil engineer:
Ing. Patricio Stagno
Constructor:
Renato Rojo
Client:
Alvaro Buzeta
Plot surface:
1800 sqm
Building surface:
112 sqm

Buzeta house is a single-family summer house located to the south of Maitencillo, standing on a terrain of 1800 sqm (19,400 sqft) and perched at the top of a steep slope, 120 meters (390 feet) above the sea. Conditions in the area are excellent for paragliding, which is why the volume has been positioned to face the wind, strengthening the presence of the slope and generating spectacular views over the sea.

The volume appears from the east as an entirely opaque façade composed of a double skin of small boards, which conceals the views on arrival.

The lateral façades contain two round windows, which, together with the steep slope on the western flank and the sea in the background, conjure up the image of a ship. The main façade leans toward the ocean revealing stunning panoramic views through a huge window, which allows the changing natural light to penetrate to the interior, throughout the course of the day. At night the roles are reversed and the interior lighting casts a soft light on the boards of the back wall, reflecting the warmth of the materials and of the house itself.

Despite the bizarre cross-section, the 112 sqm (1,200 sqft) floor plan, is perfectly rectangular and the interior is laid out symmetrically, ordered by a double-height space to which the rooms of the house are attached. A curved roof, lined with copper, inspired by the wind-swollen sails of the paragliders, runs uniformly across the house from east to west, becoming a weft of wooden boards and providing shade for the sea-facing rooms.

The materials used are Radiata pine for the structure, Oregon pine for the exterior and copper for the roofs and chimneys.

Ground floor plan

0 50 100 200 300

First floor plan

0 50 100 200 300

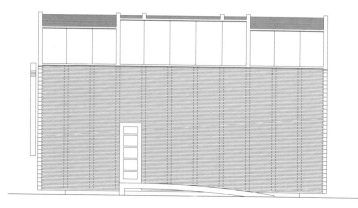

East elevation

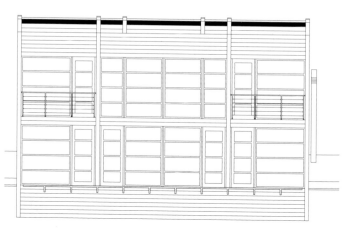

Section A

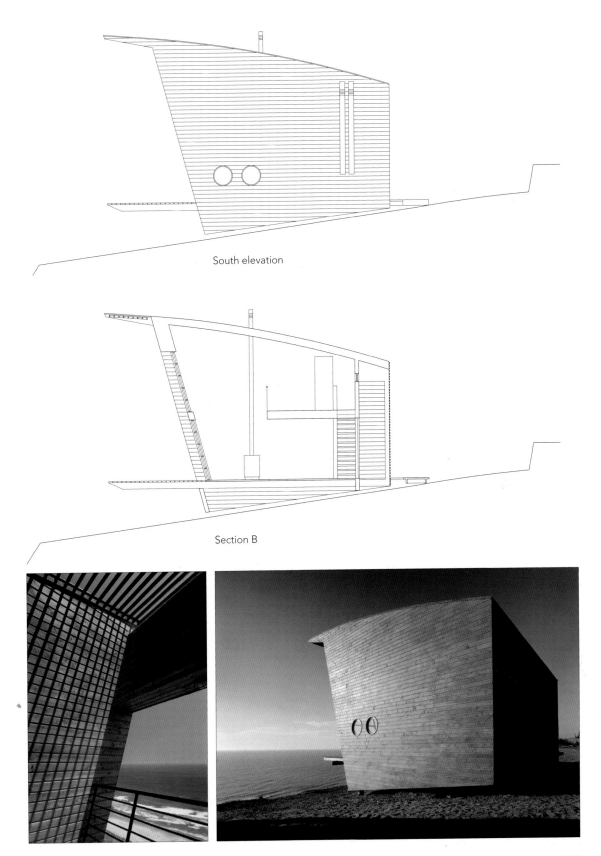

South elevation

Section B

The main façade leans toward the ocean revealing stunning panoramic views through a huge window, which allows the changing natural light to penetrate to the interior, throughout the course of the day.